Glimpses

A Study in the Parables and Signs of John

By Jason Hensley

Acknowledgments

Thanks to the brethren whose who provided invaluable feedback and encouragement for this work—Brother Bob Lloyd, Brother Tom Graham, and Brother Jim Styles.

Thanks to Brother Jason Robinson for putting together some of my rough ideas and designing the book cover.

Unless otherwise noted, all quotations are from the King James Version.

Speaking of His Glory
www.speakingofhisglory.com
July 2012

Author's Message and Introduction

This book is an in-depth look at the major signs in John's gospel. It seeks to first tell the story, and then look a bit deeper to see a parable or another meaning beneath the surface. In doing so, there are two major goals.

May this book make the Lord Jesus more real to you—that's the first goal. May this book encourage you towards the Kingdom of God and foster within you a stronger relationship with the Lord. There truly is nothing more precious than looking at the footsteps of the Master and coming to know him. May this book encourage you to this end—even if you disagree on an interpretation of one of the "parables" or if you don't even think that there is a parable beneath the story. If this book causes you to see the Lord Jesus Christ more clearly and to think more as he thought, then it will have been successful.

The other goal of this publication is to show the depth of the Word of God. The Bible is not a book which can just be read at surface level all of the time—it has a depth and a richness which is unparalleled. By looking at these parables and at the signs, may that depth open up to you.

It may be wondered why another book focused on the ministry of the Lord Jesus has been published. Our community already has an abundance of excellent books on the gospels—why another one? The reason is found in a certain difference between the majority of our books and this one. The majority of the books in our community are expositional—they bring up many deep points and seek to enhance our understanding, and reading them can be very helpful to our discipleship. This book was not written to be an exposition, although it does have expositional points. This book has been written more like a *story*—trying to put pieces of the record together and fill in the gaps so that a complete picture is the end result. At times, some of the thoughts that are brought up are simply educated guesses, and it is hoped that you will take them as such. They are my conclusions after looking at a study, but they are by no means an exclusive understanding. They were given to help paint the picture, and in doing so to help you envision the scene—to help you see the Master and to help you picture his interactions. This book was not meant to be an exhaustive study of John's signs, but instead to be a book which fills the heart with a love of Christ and a desire to go back to the Word of God and learn more of him. It is meant to make the story of the Lord more real to us. It was written so that you, as the reader, can read this book and can picture him.

May the Lord bless us as we try to envision His son together.

Jason Hensley
jason@speakingofhisglory.com

Table of Contents

Forward	Page 5
1 - Water into Wine	Page 13
2 - Healing the Nobleman's Son	Page 36
3 - The Invalid	Page 63
4 - Feeding the Five Thousand	Page 89
5 - Walking on Water	Page 124
6 - The Man Born Blind	Page 149
7 - The Resurrection of Lazarus	Page 178
8 - The Miracle of the Fish	Page 246
Epilogue	Page 275

Forward

This consideration of parables is slightly different than one which is typically found in our community. Often when you think of a parable, your mind immediately jumps to the parable of the sower, the wheat and the tares, or the vineyard. All of these are perfect examples of stories that the Lord Jesus told—but interestingly, none of them are found in the gospel of John.

In fact, we can try to list out many of our favorite, or most familiar parables—and none of them will be found in the fourth gospel. The parable of the sower, the net, the mustard seed, the marriage banquet, the vineyard, the fig tree, all of these are absent from the record of John. And when you sit down with your Bible and read through John's gospel, you will be hard pressed to find anything that even resembles a parable. Possibly you could look at the grain of wheat in John 12, or the vine in John 15, but those are quite different from the typical parables. Yet apart from those, it doesn't seem as though John's gospel has any parables.

Looking even deeper, the typical word for parable—Strong's number G3850—is never used in the gospel of John. If you do a search on that Greek word, you will notice that it occurs in Matthew, Mark, and also Luke—yet then when you come to John, the results are blank. John never used the Greek word for "parable" in his gospel. Occasionally he used the word for "proverb" (G3942), which was translated as "parable" in John 10:6, but this doesn't really seem to describe the same type of thing. A proverb and a parable are quite different—and the use in John 10 is about the good shepherd, which is more of an analogy than a story, putting it in the same category as the grain of wheat in John 12 and the vine in John 15. At first glance, the gospel of John seems almost totally void of parables.

Yet this isn't the case.

Rather, as is almost always the case with John, he set out to show things a little bit differently than Matthew, and Mark, and Luke.

John will tell parables, but they won't be stories that are told by the Lord. Instead, John's parables are found in the experiences of individuals peppered throughout his record. They are *living parables*. His parables are shown through people who come face to face with the Lord. They are stories, just as all of the other parables—yet at the same time, they are based upon real people and real events. Just like the parables in the other gospels, each of these stories has a surface level meaning and a deeper meaning. The Lord Jesus explained this feature of parables to his disciples after telling the parable of the sower:

> "And the disciples came, and said unto him, Why speakest thou unto them in parables? He answered and said unto them, Because it is given unto you to know the mysteries of the kingdom of heaven, but to them it is not given. For whosoever hath to him shall be given, and he shall have more abundance: but whosoever hath not, from him shall be taken away even that he hath. Therefore speak I to them in parables: because they seeing see not; and hearing they hear not, neither do they understand." Matthew 13:10-13

When the disciples asked the Master why he spoke to the multitude in parables, he answered by explaining that there were two classes of people:

1. The disciples, who understood the mysteries
2. The multitude, who had closed their ears and closed their eyes

Christ spoke in parables, because there were two groups listening to him—there was one group, the disciples, who would come to him and desire to know more. They would ask questions and try to understand what the parable meant (Matthew 13:36). For them, they could understand the meaning of the parable because they were searching for it—they wanted to know. Yet the multitude was different. Many of them had shut their eyes and closed their ears (Matthew 13:15). They didn't want to know. Therefore, when they heard the parable, they wouldn't search for a meaning. They would simply hear a story, and that was it. Parables were stories with a deeper meaning—that deeper meaning would be found for those who searched.

So it is in the gospel of John. His parables are stories with deeper meanings—but the stories are about real people, rather than events and circumstances described by the Lord Jesus. Just like the parables in the other gospels, the deeper meanings become apparent if only we take the time to look.

In this book, we will be looking at eight of the parables in John's gospel. Typically, these eight events are referred to as "the eight signs of John," because they are the major miracles of Christ which the apostle John recorded in his gospel. Each of them has a deeper meaning beneath the miracle, as will be seen as this book proceeds. These eight signs are as follows:

1. *Turning the water into wine*
2. *Healing the nobleman's son*
3. *Healing the invalid*
4. *Feeding the five thousand*
5. *Walking on the water*
6. *Healing the man born blind*
7. *Raising Lazarus from the dead*
8. *The one hundred and fifty-three fish*

In all of John's gospel, the Lord Jesus Christ only performed eight *major* miracles. There are others, such as appearing in a room with shut doors (John 20:19, 26), but these eight are the main miracles. All of them have a parable beneath them. In addition, all of them were recorded for a specific purpose, as John wrote at the end of his gospel. Each of the parables focus on this same purpose—showing that the Lord Jesus Christ is the Son of God and that only through him can one have life:

> "And many other signs truly did Jesus in the presence of his disciples, which are not written in this book: but these are written, that ye might believe that Jesus is the Christ, the Son of God; and that believing ye might have life through his name." John 20:30-31

John's purpose in writing these signs was twofold—he wanted his readers to hear of these miracles and in so doing, believe that Jesus is the Christ. Building upon that first purpose, his second purpose was to bring his readers to that point of acknowledging Christ as the Son of God, so that they could have life in Christ's name.

When looking at all of the signs, it can be seen how John's twofold purpose was fulfilled. Every one of these miracles proved that the Lord Jesus was the Messiah, the Son of God. They were things which no one had ever done before. No one had ever been able to give sight to one who was blind from birth. No one had ever raised someone from the dead after they had been dead for four days. These were things which only the Son of God could do. Thus, John focused on eight of Christ's miracles because these miracles were ones which specifically showed that he was the Messiah. By showing that, John's hope was that his readers would come to know the Truth and that through their knowledge, they would be led to life in the Lord.

The purpose remains the same when one looks at the deeper meaning as well—at the parable beneath the story. Hidden under each of these signs is a parable which reinforces that same message, but it focuses on the second half of John's purpose. The deeper message seeks to show that *life* is found in him—"that believing, ye might have life through his name." All of these parables show and revolve around the fact that the Lord Jesus is the Lord of life. In examining the parables, we will see that the Lord Jesus had come to bring new teaching and to free the people from their traditions and rituals—he would bring them life from dead works. We will see the reaction of various groups to his message of life. We will see pictures of different events, such as his sacrifice—in which his life was given for the life of his followers. We will see a picture of the resurrection—the giving of life to his followers who have fallen asleep. All of these parables come together to show a consistent picture. Life is found in the Lord Jesus Christ—whether or not we accept it.

"I am come that they might have life, and that they might have it more abundantly…" John 10:30

May this be true for all of us. As we look through these parables and signs, may we too be convicted by what we read. May we have a firm and solid understanding that the Lord Jesus is our Messiah, and in so believing, may we too have life in his name.

Chapter 1
The Water into Wine

The ministry of the Lord Jesus Christ had begun. That very week, he had just started to call his disciples—and now, at the end of the week, he was in a city named Cana with those whom he had called. A major miracle was about to take place, yet it would be hidden from the eyes of almost everyone present. Only a select few would know and would see the power of the Master. The apostle John witnessed this show of glory, and he recorded this sign so that many others throughout the ages could experience this first miracle of the Lord Jesus. As he wrote, he began the story with information that demands a greater context:

> "And the third day there was a marriage in Cana of Galilee; and the mother of Jesus was there." John 2:1

On the third day, there was a marriage in Cana and Mary was there. This first sentence creates questions—the third day of what? And why did John want his readers to know specifically that this was the third day?

The answers to these questions can be found in the context of the story—in John 1. There, the apostle John meticulously recorded the chronology of the first few days of Christ's ministry.

The First Few Days

Throughout John 1, the first few days of Christ's ministry are specifically recorded. The chapter opens with an introduction, and then jumps into the events of the first day. After finishing those events, John then moved on to the next day:

> "The next day John seeth Jesus coming unto him, and saith, Behold the Lamb of God, which taketh away the sin of the world." John 1:29

The events of verses 29-34 are all the events of the second day of John's gospel. After that final verse, John mentioned the third day:

> "Again the next day after John stood, and two of his disciples." John 1:35

Finally, after going through the activities of the third day, John wrote of the fourth day:

> "The day following Jesus would go forth into Galilee, and findeth Philip, and saith unto him, Follow me." John 1:43

John 1 records the events of four days. Then, the next chapter begins with the words "And the third day,"—meaning, after three more days. This interpretation is likely correct, because the Lord had not yet arrived in Cana by the actual third day of the week. "The third day," therefore, probably refers to *three days later*. Thus, when the reader arrives at John 2, they are looking at the seventh day of the record. The first four days are in John 1 and three more have passed before John 2. On the seventh day in the gospel of John, the Lord Jesus was at a marriage.

> "And the third day there was a marriage in Cana of Galilee; and the mother of Jesus was there." John 2:1

John explained that this miracle took place on the seventh day of Christ's ministry. The Lord's disciples were new—in fact, based off of chapter 1, it doesn't even seem as though he has called all of his disciples yet. Christ was there, probably with James and John, Peter and Andrew, and then Philip and Nathaniel. In addition to those disciples, Mary was also at the wedding.

Wedding of Relatives

Thus, this miracle took place very early in the preaching of the Lord, before all of the disciples were called, and the apostle found it needful to tell his readers that Mary was also at the wedding. Yet, not only was she there, but it appears as though she had a leading role in the planning and facilitating of this banquet. Somehow, Mary knew that the wine had run out:

> "And when they wanted wine, the mother of Jesus saith unto him, They have no wine." John 2:3

Mary knew that they had run out of wine. This wouldn't have been common knowledge—not even the ruler of the feast knew. Thus, she was probably one of the ones organizing the food and drink for this celebration. Yet her influence not only extended over the food, but she also seemed to have authority over the servants. After she spoke to Christ about the wine running out, she turned to the servants and commanded them to follow her son's directions:

> "His mother saith unto the servants, Whatsoever he saith unto you, do it." John 2:5

It appears as though Mary was in some type of influential and organizational position. She knew what was happening behind the scenes at the wedding, and she had authority over the servants. The fact that Mary was in this position perhaps indicates that this was a wedding of one of Jesus' relatives, or a close family friend. Someone close to Mary was getting married, and thus Mary was involved in organizing the celebration. This idea is further established when it is recognized that Cana is a town that is just a few miles north of Nazareth—not far at all from where Jesus grew up. On top of that, in verse 2, John went on to tell his readers that Jesus and his disciples were invited to this marriage:

> "And both Jesus was called, and his disciples, to the marriage." John 2:2

The Lord Jesus and his disciples were invited to the wedding—the bride or groom must have had some kind of connection to either him or his family. Thus, the Lord Jesus was at a family wedding or the wedding of a family friend, and the wine had run out. His mother had come to him and divulged the problem—just imagine what an embarrassment it could be to her, the one organizing everything, if all of the guests found out that the wine had run out!

Christ's Answer to His Mother

Throughout his years in his mother's house, Christ had probably come to show wisdom and resourcefulness in all aspects of life, and so Mary trusted that he would develop a clever solution to the problem. It's doubtful that she expected him to perform a miracle—John wrote that the water into wine was his *first* miracle (John 2:11). Instead, upon this belief in his resourcefulness, Mary came to her son and told him of the problem. Little did she know how he would respond. She likely expected him to immediately jump into action, to take control of the situation and quickly remedy the problem. Instead, she was given an unexpected reply:

> "Jesus saith unto her, Woman, what have I to do with thee? mine hour is not yet come." John 2:4

What did this mean? Why was her son not working immediately to help her? Perhaps she thought that she just didn't understand what he meant—one can almost see the confusion on her face as she heard his response to her plea. The answer of the Lord doesn't seem to be connected to the question. She asked him to solve a problem about the wine at this wedding, and he responded by speaking about his "hour." Yet as is often the case—especially in the writings of John—the Lord Jesus Christ's words were spoken on a totally different level than the words which were said to him. Truly they did answer the question, but often the hearers didn't realize the connection.

"Woman, what have I do to with thee?" Most assuredly, this was not a harsh or disrespectful answer. In modern times, it would seem so—never would a loving or respectful son refer to his mother as "woman." However, it was different for the Lord Jesus Christ—this is the same title with which he addressed his mother when he was on the cross (John 19:26), and undoubtedly in that instance it was spoken with much grace and care. Surely, it was the same here. When the Master called his mother "woman," it was spoken respectfully and lovingly. Yet it is important to note that while it was spoken gently, it was not "mother."

This was the point that the Lord was driving home. To him, she was no longer "mother" (cp. Matthew 12:46-50). His ministry was beginning—from this point on, he was not the son of Mary. He was the Son of God. He would be about his Father's business for the rest of his life—this earthly family was no longer his primary family. This is why John continually referred to her as the Lord's "mother" in this account, yet Christ never referred to her as such—the apostle was purposefully showing the contrast. She *was* his mother, but the Master did not refer to her as such.

Instead, the Lord Jesus was drawing out a deeper lesson. Things had changed now that his ministry had begun—he had a greater focus—that focus was ultimately the glory of his Father, which would come to a focal point on the cross. That is what was meant by "my hour has not yet come." Constantly throughout the gospel of John, Christ's "hour," is a reference to the crucifixion.

> "Then they sought to take him: but no man laid hands on him, because his hour was not yet come." John 7:30

Though the religious leaders sought to take hold of Christ, they could not capture him—because it was not yet his hour. It was not the time for the cross. Again, this same term is used in the same way in John 8.

> "These words spake Jesus in the treasury, as he taught in the temple: and no man laid hands on him; for his hour was not yet come." John 8:20

Water into Wine

The Lord spoke and taught openly, yet no one took hold of him—because it was not yet his hour. Another example of this term is found at the account of the Last Supper. Then, his hour had finally come.

> "Now before the feast of the passover, when Jesus knew that <u>his hour was come</u> that he should depart out of this world unto the Father, having loved his own which were in the world, he loved them unto the end." John 13:1

Christ's "hour" was a reference to his crucifixion. That was now his ultimate focus. "Woman, what have I to do with thee?"—relationships had changed. His focus was different. He was journeying to the cross. All of the language that he used pointed to this—in all of Scripture, the only other time that he referred to Mary as "woman" was when he was hanging on the cross:

> "When Jesus therefore saw his mother, and the disciple standing by, whom he loved, he saith unto his mother, <u>Woman</u>, behold thy son!" John 19:26

As far as can be seen, this was the only other time that the Lord referred to his mother in this way. Thus, when he said this to her from the cross, what might her mind have flashed back to?—Quite possibly, her mind went to the water into wine. She must have remembered the miracle, and as he said this from the cross, she probably realized what he had meant three years earlier. So often that was the case in the gospels—Jesus said or did something and people didn't truly understand it until years later (John 2:22, Luke 24:6-8). Christ's focus was no longer on his earthly family. He was focused on his Father, which meant that his eyes were fixed on the cross. His life was now about preaching the Kingdom of

God, not about intervening to help his mother when they had run out of wine at a wedding. His mission was higher, it was greater, and ultimately would take him to Calvary.

The Waterpots

Thus Mary, probably slightly bewildered by what her son had said to her, turned to the servants, still believing that Jesus would help her; he had never failed her before:

> "His mother saith unto the servants, Whatsoever he saith unto you, do it." John 2:5

His mother had given the order to the servants—but what would the Lord do? Would he decide to come up with a solution? Though his words intimated that he might not, yet his mother hadn't understood. So, in an act of love towards Mary and with the glory of his Father in mind (John 2:11), the Lord Jesus took this opportunity to act out a parable. He would help his earthly family and still focus on the honor of his Father. Thus, he began his instructions:

> "And there were set there six waterpots of stone, after the manner of the purifying of the Jews, containing two or three firkins apiece. Jesus saith unto them, Fill the waterpots with water. And they filled them up to the brim." John 2:6-7

There were six waterpots, and Jesus commanded that all six of them be filled. Newer translations help to show just what a great task this was that the Lord required:

Water into Wine

"Now there were set there six waterpots of stone, according to the manner of purification of the Jews, containing <u>twenty or thirty gallons</u> apiece." John 2:6 NKJV

"Now there were six stone water jars there for the Jewish rites of purification, each holding <u>twenty or thirty gallons</u>." John 2:6 ESV

"Now there were six stone waterpots set there for the Jewish custom of purification, containing <u>twenty or thirty gallons</u> each." John 2:6 NASB

These pots could each hold twenty or thirty gallons—they were by no means small! They were fairly good sized pots, and the Lord commanded the servants to fill them to the brim. One can just picture the servants taking their small pitcher of water, pouring it into the pot, and then going back to get more water. Again and again this happened until the pots were filled. The loyal servants fulfilled the command by the Lord Jesus. Then, after this great task was finished, the Master gave them an even greater command:

> "And he saith unto them, Draw out now, and bear unto the governor of the feast. And they bare it." John 2:8

The pots were filled and the Lord commanded them to take the water to the ruler of the feast! Just imagine that! The servants had just spent the last few minutes trying to fill up these large pots with water, and then they were supposed to bring it to the ruler of the feast—which creates a bit of a question. When did the water actually turn into wine? Did it become wine while it was in the waterpots? Or did it become wine as soon as the servants poured it for the governor? When did the water change into wine? It's difficult to say the exact moment that the water was transformed, but certainly it was still water when the servants drew it out to give it to the ruler of the feast. Notice the little detail which John gave:

> "When the ruler of the feast had tasted the water that was made wine, and knew not whence it was: (but the servants <u>which drew the water</u> knew;) the governor of the feast called the bridegroom…" John 2:9

"The servants which drew *the water* knew." The Scriptural record doesn't say, "the servants which drew the wine knew"—meaning that it was still water when it was drawn out! The phrase "drew the water" is a clear hearkening back to Christ's command to "draw out" and give to the ruler. This detail wasn't referring to when the servants filled up the jars, it was referring to when they drew out and gave to the governor! Imagine the faith of these servants in the words of Christ! He had just told them to take a pitcher of water to the ruler of the feast! Yet the servants did it—and their faith was rewarded as they saw the water turn into wine!

The faith of these servants is extraordinary—who would have that type of faith in the Lord? This was Christ's first miracle! He had never before done anything like this. To add to that, it was only the first week of his ministry—no one had yet heard of him. To the people, he was merely the carpenter's son. But these servants had absolute trust and faith in him—they were willing to bring the water to the governor of the feast. Why would they trust Christ so much? Who would have this kind of faith in the Master at this early stage?

The Servants

It's an interesting thought to ponder—why did the servants have such faith in the Lord Jesus Christ? Perhaps it can be answered when some intriguing clues are considered. As it would seem, the only people who would have had this much faith in the Master would have been the disciples. The proclamations which they made of the Lord in the prior chapter demonstrate their trust in him.

When Andrew met the Lord Jesus, he ran to his brother Peter to tell him about the Lord. This is what he said:

> "We have found the Mesias, which is, being interpreted, the Christ." John 1:41

Already, even in this early stage of the Lord's ministry, he was Andrew's Messiah. The next day, when Philip went to tell Nathaniel of the Lord Jesus, this is what he said of him:

> "We have found him, of whom Moses in the law, and the prophets, did write, Jesus of Nazareth, the son of Joseph." John 1:45

For Philip, his belief in Christ was similar to Andrew's. From the very beginning, he knew that the Master was the fulfillment of the prophecies. Nathaniel said something similar:

> "Rabbi, thou art the Son of God; thou art the King of Israel." John 1:49

Glimpses of the Master

When speaking to the Master himself, Nathaniel voiced his belief that Jesus was the son of God—the King of Israel. These disciples were the men who believed in the Lord Jesus. Even before he had performed a miracle, they were willing to devote their lives to him because they believed that he was the Anointed of God, the only begotten. These were the men who would follow him, even if they did not understand his commands. If he told them to take water and bring it to the governor, they would do it. Because of their belief in him, they would follow and they would serve. Could it be that when the record refers to the "servants" it is actually referring to the disciples?

Looking at some of the evidence, it seems quite possible. If this was a wedding of someone related to the Lord Jesus, they probably would not have had the money to have hired servants. Remember that Christ came from a financially humble family. When he was born, Mary brought the poorest offering to the temple. The wine had probably run out because the family didn't have the money to buy enough. The servants would not have been hired servants. Instead, the servants and those who were in charge of the wedding were probably people who were known by the family and who were willing to help, such as Mary. In addition, this connection between the disciples and the servants also helps to explain why the disciples believed on Christ after the miracle:

> "This beginning of miracles did Jesus in Cana of Galilee, and manifested forth his glory; <u>and his disciples believed on him.</u>" John 2:11

The disciples somehow saw the glory of Christ in all of this. How? Unless they had been part of the group who was taking part in the miracle, how would they have known that the wine had run out in the first place, let alone that a miracle had happened? The wine running out was something secret, no one knew about it! Christ's mother came to him and disclosed the problem—but she would not have wanted others to know. It would have been an embarrassment. Yet somehow, the disciples were able to recognize that a miracle had taken place—possibly because they had been personally involved.

As a final point towards the understanding that the disciples were the servants, there is an interesting match between the amount of disciples and the amount of the waterpots. There were six waterpots—and surprisingly, there seem to have been six disciples at this point. In John 1, the Lord Jesus called Andrew and John—and the way that the record is worded, it sounds as though John and Andrew both went to call their brothers. Thus, James and Peter joined the group. Then, on the next day, the Lord called Philip and Nathaniel—making six disciples. Therefore, when the Lord came to Cana with his disciples, there were six of them. Six disciples for the six waterpots.

The evidence comes together fairly well and helps to create a full picture. By bringing together all of these pieces, the story can become more real.

It was the first week of Christ's ministry. The wine had run out at a wedding of someone related to or close to the Lord Jesus. Christ was asked to help, but he told his mother that things were changing, and his focus was now the cross. She didn't understand and asked his disciples to help Christ solve the problem. The six waterpots were filled, the water was drawn out and taken to the governor of the feast, and he made proclamation that this wine was better than the first.

The Parable

But beneath all of this there seems to be a deeper meaning—and the indications of this deeper meaning begin right at the commencement of John's gospel:

> "In the beginning was the Word, and the Word was with God, and the Word was God." John 1:1

"In the beginning..." There is another book in Scripture that begins this way—and it would appear as though John's use of the phrase was a purposeful allusion back to Genesis. After beginning his gospel in the same way, John then went on to write about the first seven days of the Lord's ministry? The first seven days—there's another book in Scripture that begins that same way—again, the book of Genesis. John purposefully put these connections into his gospel, so that when his readers began to go through it, their minds would automatically be taken back to Genesis and the seven days of creation.

Notice, then, that in the Genesis account the seventh day was the day in which God rested—and in the 7000 year plan, the final thousand years represents that millennium in which there will be a rest for the people of God. This rest will be ushered in by an event known as the marriage of the lamb—when the Lord Jesus is beautifully united with his bride. This wedding takes place at the beginning of the seventh millennium—that time of rest. Suddenly, when putting these things together, it becomes apparent that it is no coincidence that John brought his readers back to Genesis, connected their minds to the day of rest and the marriage of the lamb, and then wrote that Christ, on the seventh day, was called to a marriage.

There's a deliberate connection that the apostle was making, and he wanted his readers to realize that this whole parable is focused on the Kingdom of God and the marriage of the lamb. This is perhaps the reason that the first chapter mentions twice that Jesus is the "lamb of God":

> "The next day John seeth Jesus coming unto him, and saith, Behold the Lamb of God, which taketh away the sin of the world." John 1:29

Just a few verses later, John again called the Master the same thing:

> "And looking upon Jesus as he walked, he saith, Behold the Lamb of God!" John 1:36

When writing the beginning of his gospel, John, guided by the Spirit, specifically used language which connected this wedding in Cana with the "marriage of the lamb." Not only is the Lord Jesus called the "Lamb of God" twice in John 1, but even the language used about the marriage in Cana has overtones that connect it to the marriage of the lamb. Notice the way that the readers are told about Christ's presence at the wedding:

> "And both Jesus was called, and his disciples, to the marriage." John 2:2

Note the specific words that John used. He didn't say that Jesus and his disciples "were there," as he said of

Mary in the first verse, but he intentionally used the words "called" and "marriage," connecting these words to ones which he would later write in the book of Revelation:

> "And he saith unto me, Write, Blessed are they which are <u>called</u> unto the <u>marriage</u> supper of the Lamb. And he saith unto me, These are the true sayings of God." Revelation 19:9

"Blessed are they which are called to the marriage…" Jesus and his disciples were *called* to the *marriage*. The apostle sought to make a connection between the wedding at Cana and the marriage of the lamb. Thus, in the parable, this wedding represents the Kingdom of God.

Yet at the same time, while the weddings is a picture of the Kingdom of God, it is also a picture of a marriage in which the guests were in jeopardy of losing their feast, because the wine had run out. The problem was solved by the Lord Jesus, and he, by filling six waterpots with living water, created new wine, which was better than the first and allowed a full and wonderful marriage celebration to take place. *If the Lord Jesus had not intervened*, the guests at the wedding would not have been able to celebrate in this picture of the marriage of the lamb.

This was the first miracle performed by the Lord, and it took place at the beginning of his ministry. In effect, its parabolic meaning would sum up the work which he had come to do. The people of God were in jeopardy of losing their place in the Kingdom. Their corruption of the law and their reliance upon the statutes of Moses, rather than its principles, had led them to a position in which their old doctrine, or old wine, had essentially failed. To provide a solution, the Lord Jesus would fill his six disciples (and more later) with living water, and they would fill the world with the new and better wine—the superior doctrine of Christ. In doing so, this doctrine would allow the marriage feast to continue, or allow its followers to find a place at the marriage of the Lamb.

Superiority to the Law

The first indication that this miracle is connected to the deadness of the law is found in the literal rendering of the phrase "when they wanted wine" (John 2:3). This phrase is better translated as "when the wine failed." A number of different translations translate it as such:

> "When the wine failed, the mother of Jesus said to him, 'They have no wine.'" John 2:3 RSV

> "And when the wine failed, the mother of Jesus saith unto him, They have no wine." John 2:3 ASV

> "And wine having failed, the mother of Jesus saith unto him, 'Wine they have not.'" John 2:3 YLT

The old wine had failed—and wine can typically represent doctrine and teaching (Matthew 26:27-28, Revelation 14:8). Here, this wine represented the doctrines of the Jews; it showed their traditions and rituals—their corrupted form of the law. These traditions were empty and dead. They were supposed to lead people to God, but they did nothing of the kind. Instead, they were heavy burdens on the people which they could not bear (Matthew 23:4). In no way could they bring life and in no way could they bring joy. They created a system which could only lead to death. This was stressed by the writer to the Hebrews when he referred to the works of the law as "dead" works:

> "Therefore leaving the principles of the doctrine of Christ, let us go on unto perfection ; not laying again the foundation of <u>repentance from dead works</u>, and of faith toward God…" Hebrews 6:1

The writer wrote about repenting from the dispensation that the Hebrew believers were under before—the dead works. The principles beneath the law had become totally obscured by the Jews' traditions. Thus, the law became a set of dead rules and dead works. The wine failed. The writer said this same thing again, just a few chapters later.

> "How much more shall the blood of Christ, who through the eternal Spirit offered himself without spot to God, <u>purge your conscience from dead works</u> to serve the living God?" Hebrews 9:14

The works of the law were dead, and they could not lead to salvation—even after following the works, the conscience still needed to be purged. In other words, trying to find a place in the Kingdom marriage through works would only lead to death. The works failed. But thankfully, a solution to this corruption of Moses could be found in the Lord Jesus Christ.

The Waterpots

To allow the people of God to still find a place in the marriage feast, the Master would fill up six waterpots with water—six pots for the six disciples. This is the first connection between the waterpots and the disciples—a further can be made when it is noted that the waterpots were made of stone. Later in the New Testament, the disciples and all of the followers of Christ were referred to as "earthen vessels."

> "But we have this treasure in earthen vessels, that the excellency of the power may be of God, and not of us." 2 Corinthians 4:7

The followers of Christ were "earthen vessels." So it is in the parable—these six waterpots represent the first six followers of the Lord Jesus Christ. The traditions of the Jews and the works of the law had failed; but Christ would fill his disciples with living water, and that water would go forth from them and become new wine—wine which was better than the first. No longer would these waterpots be used for the purifying of the law, but in fact they would be used to bring true purification—purification of the heart to all of the world.

> "Who gave himself for us, that he might redeem us from all iniquity, and purify unto himself a peculiar people, zealous of good works." Titus 2:14

These disciples would go forth throughout the world to purify a special people for God. They would do this through the living water with which they had been filled.

From Water to Wine

Later in his gospel, John would give a clear indication of what this living water represented:

Glimpses of the Master

"In the last day, that great day of the feast, Jesus stood and cried, saying, If any man thirst, let him come unto me, and drink. He that believeth on me, as the scripture hath said, out of his belly shall flow <u>rivers of living water. (But this spake he of the Spirit</u>, which they that believe on him should receive: for the Holy Spirit was not yet given; because that Jesus was not yet glorified.)" John 7:37-39

Christ referred to the gift of the Holy Spirit as "living water"! These gifts had not yet been given because Jesus had not yet been raised, but after his resurrection, the living water poured forth from his followers. Once the Master was glorified, this living water filled up his disciples, just as it did the waterpots:

"And when he had said this, he breathed on them, and saith unto them, <u>Receive ye the Holy Spirit</u>." John 20:22

The living water was poured into the disciples and subsequently, it flowed forth from them. As the water passed out of the disciples into the rest of the world, it became that new wine—that new teaching of Christ! This Lord Jesus said this to his disciples later in his ministry:

"But when they deliver you up, take no thought how or what ye shall speak: for it shall be given you in that same hour what ye shall speak. <u>For it is not ye that speak, but the Spirit of your Father which speaketh in you.</u>" Matthew 10:19-20

When the disciples were brought before rulers and kings, they did not need to worry about what they would say—the Spirit filled them with wisdom and they knew exactly what words to speak. The Spirit which filled them, that living water, "became" the doctrine of Christ. Again, there was an intimate connection between the Spirit and this new wine, the teaching of the Master:

> "And they were all filled with the Holy Spirit, and began to speak with other tongues, as the Spirit gave them utterance." Acts 2:4

When the Holy Spirit came upon the apostles, they all began to speak forth the things of God. Just as the water changed to wine after it had left the waterpots, so it was with the Holy Spirit. It filled the apostles, and as they spread the Truth, it gave them thoughts and it gave them words to speak—the new wine or the new doctrine of the Lord Jesus Christ.

All together, this parable shows a scene in which the traditions of the Jews had failed. Their failure resulted in an inability to bring their adherents to a joyful celebration in the marriage supper of the Kingdom of God. Yet in God's mercy, the Lord Jesus created a way to save the celebration. He would fill his six disciples with the Holy Spirit, and this Spirit would lead them in preaching the new doctrine of Christ—the new wine.

Christ's way was better than the old way. The traditions could only bring death, yet Christ could bring life. His new teaching could keep the celebration alive and possible for the guests. His way was better than the corrupted law which the Jews feverishly followed. This was affirmed by the words of the governor of the feast:

> "The governor of the feast called the bridegroom, and saith unto him, Every man at the beginning doth set forth good wine; and when men have well drunk,

then that which is worse: <u>but thou hast kept the good wine until now.</u>" John 2:9-10

This new wine was greater than any wine which had come before it. This new wine was the teaching of the Lord Jesus Christ.

New Wine

The purpose of this parable was to confirm the superiority of Christ's teaching over the traditions of the Pharisees. The Lord actually proved this interpretation of the parable to his disciples just a few days after the miracle had taken place.

Luke 5 is in the context of the first week or week and a half of Christ's ministry (see Luke 4:16 and Luke 6:1), thus it comes almost directly after the wedding in Cana. During this time, the scribes and Pharisees came to Christ and asked him a question about the law:

> "And they said unto him, Why do the disciples of John fast often, and make prayers, and likewise the disciples of the Pharisees; but thine eat and drink?" Luke 5:33

Essentially they were asking him, "why do your disciples not follow the traditions? Why are they not fasting?" In his answer to them, the Lord alluded back to this first miracle, and he spoke about his teaching as "new wine." His answer was twofold. First:

> "Can ye make the children of the bridechamber fast, while the bridegroom is with them? But the days will come, when the bridegroom shall be taken away

from them, and then shall they fast in those days." Luke 5:34-35

In the context of why they did not celebrate the law, the Lord used the analogy of a wedding! The disciples had *just* been at a wedding, only days prior. Their minds would have flashed back to the miracle that Christ had performed. And the answer to Christ's question was clear—of course the children of the bridechamber don't fast while they are with the bridegroom! This was supposed to be a time of celebration!

Yet perhaps as they thought over the Lord's question, the disciples remembered they they almost *had seen* the guests fasting at a wedding—because the wine had failed! Christ then continued his answer, and notice the analogy that he chose to use. This was not an accident!

> "And he spake also a parable unto them; No man putteth a piece of a new garment upon an old; if otherwise, then both the new maketh a rent, and the piece that was taken out of the new agreeth not with the old. And no man putteth new wine into old bottles; else the new wine will burst the bottles, and be spilled, and the bottles shall perish." Luke 5:36-37

The Lord explained again that his disciples did not follow the law of fasting because new wine doesn't go into an old wineskin. New teaching doesn't fit into the mold of the old teaching. Things were changing—something new was coming. A new wine, or a new doctrine was coming. Again, immediately the disciples minds would flash back to the wedding, where Jesus had made new wine—and and in which he had demonstrated his superiority and his glory (John 2:11).

Glimpses of the Master
Understanding the Point

This parable shows a picture of salvation. It tells the story of Christ's mission. The feverish following of the works of the law could never bring life in the Kingdom. They were dead works. The old wine failed—it had come to teach principles, yet the people mistakingly thought that it could earn them eternal life.

In an act of mercy, Yahweh sent His son to provide for the failing wine. The Lord Jesus filled his six disciples with living water, the Holy Spirit—and through the Holy Spirit, they brought the new wine of Christ to the rest of the world. This first miracle of the Lord declared his purpose. He had come to seek and save that which was lost, that which was floundering under the failing system of traditions.

For many of us, this lesson can tend to get lost. We don't live under the law and we don't have a group of religious rulers seeking to enforce a strict following of the commandments. It can be easy to lose the significance of the lesson, and just take our freedom in Christ for granted. Yet each one of us needs the reminder. We live by principle, not by rules and tradition. We have been set at liberty and have been filled with the new wine. We can recognize that this wine is much better than the first. We are no longer bound by the regulations of men, but instead are charged with filling ourselves with the Word of God and feasting upon the new wine of Christ. In doing this, we can let the principles of God guide our lives and our thoughts.

For this liberty, for this knowledge, and for His principles, we should be thankful.

Chapter 2
Healing the Nobleman's Son

The Lord Jesus had miraculously turned the water into wine, and from there, he went down to Jerusalem. While at Jerusalem, he turned over the tables of the moneychangers and cast them out of the temple. After these events, many people were impressed with the Master. In him, they saw a man who had the courage to charge into the temple and push out the moneychangers—someone who was willing to stand up against the established power. On top of that, they also saw a man who had the power to perform miracles:

> "Now when he was in Jerusalem at the passover, in the feast day, many believed in his name, <u>when they saw the miracles which he did</u>." John 2:23

All throughout this time, people had been looking for the promised Messiah (Luke 3:15). They were looking for one who would deliver them from the oppression of the Romans. They were expecting a miracle worker and one who would have the power to stand up against their mighty foe. Because of what they had seen at the Passover, many began to believe on Christ—even some of the Pharisees were impressed.

> "There was a man of the Pharisees, named Nicodemus, a ruler of the Jews: the same came to Jesus by night, and said unto him, Rabbi, we know that thou art a teacher come from God: <u>for no man can do these miracles that thou doest</u>, except God be with him." John 3:1-2

Healing the Nobleman's Son

Nicodemus was one of the Pharisees that believed on Christ—yet at this point, his belief was based upon the fact that the Lord could perform miracles. All throughout the land, the popularity of the Lord Jesus Christ rose because of the mighty works which he could do. Those who were blind could see again! Those who were lame could now walk! The people had never seen anything like this before; by the end of his ministry, many had begun to flock to him simply because of the miracles:

> "After these things Jesus went over the sea of Galilee, which is the sea of Tiberias. And a great multitude followed him, because they saw his miracles which he did on them that were diseased."
> John 6:1-2

Because of the miracles, a great multitude began to follow the Lord—but this particular type of popular acclaim was not what he desired. The Master healed people as a gift for their faith (Matthew 9:22) and as a taste of wonders of the kingdom of God (Luke 11:20). Christ did not want to gain the reputation of a mere miracle worker, and he also did not want to arouse the suspicion of the religious rulers—especially at the beginning of his ministry. This was why he constantly told the people whom he healed to keep quiet about their healing:

> "And as soon as he had spoken, immediately the leprosy departed from him, and he was cleansed. And he straightly charged him, and forthwith sent him away; and saith unto him, <u>See thou say nothing to any man</u>: but go thy way, shew thyself to the priest, and offer for thy cleansing those things which

Moses commanded, for a testimony unto them."
Mark 1:42-44

After the Lord cleansed this leper, he "straightly charged him" and told him not to speak of his healing to others! In another incident recorded by Matthew, Christ said the same type of thing:

> "But when Jesus knew it, he withdrew himself from thence: and great multitudes followed him, and he healed them all; and charged them that they should not make him known." Matthew 12:15-16

Again, the Lord Jesus healed many who were sick and charged them not to spread the word about his miraculous works! At first this policy may seem strange, but it had a twofold purpose—to prevent the multitude from coming to him just because of the miracles and also to dodge the attention of the Pharisees (Matthew 12:14). Christ was not looking to be labeled as a social reformer or a revolutionary. Matthew went on to explain this:

> "That it might be fulfilled which was spoken by Esaias the prophet, saying, Behold my servant, whom I have chosen; my beloved, in whom my soul is well pleased: I will put my spirit upon him, and he shall shew judgment to the Gentiles. <u>He shall not strive, nor cry; neither shall any man hear his voice in the streets.</u>" Matthew 12:17-19

The Lord had not come looking for fame. He was not going from city to city so that he might stir up the people and gain a revolutionary following. That was not the point. Instead, the Lord Jesus had come to preach.

Healing the Nobleman's Son

He had come to teach people about the Kingdom of God and prepare them for it:

> "And he said unto them, I must preach the kingdom of God to other cities also: for therefore am I sent." Luke 4:43

Jesus was sent to preach the Kingdom of God. He did not come solely as a miracle worker, although he performed plenty of miracles. Instead, he came to teach people. Again, he said the same thing to Pilate:

> "Pilate therefore said unto him, Art thou a king then? Jesus answered, Thou sayest that I am a king. <u>To this end was I born, and for this cause came I into the world, that I should bear witness unto the truth</u>. Every one that is of the truth heareth my voice." John 18:37

The Lord Jesus came to bear witness to the Truth. Unfortunately, many people simply followed him because of the miracles. They desired to see signs and wonders. At the same time, these miracles caught the attention of the religious rulers. Such was the situation at the beginning of John 4. Many people followed the Master merely because of the sigs and wonders, and Pharisees had begun to notice this new preacher from Nazareth:

> "When therefore the Lord knew how the Pharisees had heard that Jesus made and baptized more disciples than John...he left Judaea, and departed again into Galilee." John 4:1, 3

Once the Lord heard that he was arousing the attention of the Pharisees, he left Judaea and went into Galilee.

Galilee was his own country—people there knew him and they knew his parents. There, he wouldn't have a hard time blending in and staying out of the eyes of the religious rulers. As he went, he stopped in Samaria and preached to the Samaritans. After two days, he continued on his way to his homeland:

> "Now after two days he departed thence, and went into Galilee. For Jesus himself testified, <u>that a prophet hath not honor in his own country</u>." John 4:43-44

The Lord specifically went into Galilee because it was there that he believed he would not have honor. He would not have that popular acclaim which he didn't want and which caught the attention of the Pharisees. Unfortunately, however, such would not be the case. The news of his miracles had not only spread throughout Judaea—it had also gone all throughout Galilee. Even in his own country he was known as a miracle worker.

> "Then when he was come into Galilee, the Galilaeans received him, having seen all the things that he did at Jerusalem at the feast: for they also went unto the feast." John 4:45

Even the Galilaeans had seen the amazing things which Christ did at Jerusalem. They too were impressed with him. Unfortunately for the Lord, this does not seem to be what he was wanted at the time. He had come into his own country so that he could keep a low profile, but his reputation had preceded him. More than likely, after coming to Galilee and seeing how he was received because of the miracles, he probably wished that he were back in Samaria, with those who believed on him, not because of his mighty works, but because of the words which he spake (John 4:41). Sadly this was not the case and so the Lord went back into Cana—the town where he had originally made the water into wine.

> "So Jesus came again into Cana of Galilee, where he made the water wine. And there was a certain nobleman, whose son was sick at Capernaum." John 4:46

Come Down...

The Lord Jesus had come into Cana looking for respite from the popularity. He had not come to be the revolutionary leader that many sought. He had not come simply to perform miracles. Yet even in this simple village, the Lord could not stay away from those who were looking for a sign.

A nobleman from Capernaum had come to Cana looking for Jesus. He was probably some type of royal officer—the Greek word for "nobleman" is translated as "king" in Acts 12:20, and "royal" in Acts 12:21. Often throughout the Greek Old Testament (Septuagint) it is used to denote royalty (Esther 2:23, 9:3; Job 18:14). Thus, this "nobleman" was probably a man who had a number of servants and a man who was used to giving orders. Yet he didn't send his servants on this mission. His son was sick and the situation was desperate. He went on the mission personally.

The journey from Capernaum to Cana is a little shorter than twenty miles. The nobleman would have travelled as quickly as he possibly could. The need was dire and the time was short.

> "When he heard that Jesus was come out of Judaea into Galilee, he went unto him, and besought him that he would come down, and heal his son: for he was at the point of death." John 4:47

He pleaded with the Lord to come—his son was about to die. Who knew how much worse he could have become in the last few hours? For twenty miles the man had been apart from his dying son—he had heard that there was a man who had the power to perform miracles and he was determined to get this man to come down with him to Capernaum.

Signs and Wonders

Yet this was not what the Lord Jesus wanted. His ministry wasn't just about miracles. So many had already sought to follow him because of what they had seen. He had come into Galilee for the exact purpose of leaving this "fame" and reputation—but someone else had come to him with the request for a miracle. The Lord wasn't at all bereft of compassion, but performing miracles and healing the sick was not his main purpose—if it was, he could have just healed everyone in Israel in an instant. Yet he didn't. He had come to preach the Kingdom of God. The signs and the wonders supplemented that preaching. Thus, he said to the nobleman:

> "Then said Jesus unto him, Except ye see signs and wonders, ye will not believe." John 4:48

Everyone wanted the Lord to perform signs. They all wanted to see his miracles. But miracles do not

Healing the Nobleman's Son

automatically produce faith. They can confirm faith which already exists (Mark 16:20, Hebrews 2:4), and they can cause great thankfulness when people witness them (Luke 5:25-26), but they cannot *compel* someone to believe. They *should* be enough to change us (John 10:38, John 14:11), yet they often don't break through the hardness of our hearts (John 12:37). This is apparent from the wilderness wanderings. Every single day, Israel saw a miracle as the manna appeared before them (Exodus 16:35). They drank water out of the rock. Yet their hearts were not changed (1 Corinthians 10:5; Hebrews 3:8)! This is also supported by the discourse that took place after the feeding of the five thousand. The day after the miracle, Jesus met the same multitude on the shore of the sea of Galilee:

> "Jesus answered and said unto them, This is the work of God, that ye believe on him whom he hath sent. They said therefore unto him, <u>What sign shewest thou then, that we may see, and believe thee? what dost thou work?</u>" John 6:29-30

What sign shewest thou?! This was said to Christ just one day after he had produced a meal for over five thousand people from five barley loaves and two fish! Truly, the people *had* seen a marvelous sign! Yet the miracle was not enough to bring them to a lasting faith—they believed on him the day that he performed the miracle. In fact, they believed on him so fervently that they wanted to make him their king (John 6:15). But, their belief did not last and within twenty-four hours, they forgot the greatness of the miracle. True faith never materialized. They claimed that if they saw a sign, then they would believe—yet they had just previously seen a mighty miracle, and that true belief had not come. Again, even the Lord himself taught this same thing—that miracles do not automatically produce faith—in one of his parables:

> "Abraham saith unto him, They have Moses and the prophets; let them hear them. And he said, Nay, father Abraham: but if one went unto them from the dead, they will repent. And he said unto him, <u>If they hear not Moses and the prophets, neither will they be persuaded, though one rose from the dead.</u>" Luke 16:29-31

Even if someone rose again from the dead, these men would not believe—and so it was. Soon after this parable was told, a man named Lazarus came to life again after being dead four days. Yet this amazing miracle wasn't enough to break through the rock-like hearts of the religious rulers. Still they rejected Christ. Though they would see miracles, they would not turn—yet it remained one of their claims, that if they saw a sign or wonder, then they would believe.

That was the purpose of what Christ said to the nobleman. "Except ye see signs and wonders, ye will not believe." It was almost as though the Lord was using the favorite phrase of that generation and asking the nobleman if he was the same way. Had the nobleman just come to him because he wanted to see a dose of divine power in action? Had he decided that he would believe in Christ *only* if he saw a sign? His generation was constantly looking for signs—and unless they saw some kind of miracle, they claimed that they would not believe. Was this nobleman the same? The Lord was testing this man—it sounded almost as though Christ would not heal the boy. What would the nobleman do if that were the case? Would that confirm the unbelief which already existed in his heart, or did he actually believe at that moment, *before* he had seen the miracle? Did the man have faith, or was he just like the rest of his generation?

Final Plea

It was almost as though the man completely didn't understand Christ's response. He likely wondered why the Lord's reply was about people not believing and people having to see signs. Surely he had demonstrated his belief by racing up to Cana from Capernaum! If only he could get the healer to stop delaying and come with him! Thus, he reiterated his plea:

> "The nobleman saith unto him, Sir, come down ere my child die." John 4:49

Perhaps if he emphasized the urgency, then the physician would come to him. His child was dying! The Greek word used here for "child," denotes a little boy or a little girl. His little boy was on his death bed! They needed to hurry!

Yet the man still had not shown his faith—he had shown that he believed that Jesus could heal, but Christ wanted something even deeper. Did his faith have more depth? Did he truly believe in the power of Christ?

Belief

> "Jesus saith unto him. Go thy way; thy son liveth. And the man believed the word that Jesus had spoken unto him, and he went his way." John 4:50

The man believed the word that Jesus had spoken. He had never seen a miracle, he had never seen Christ heal someone—yet he believed. Just like the Samaritans, who believed Christ's word (John 4:41), this man heard the word of Christ and believed. This was not at all what he expected the Lord to do, but his faith rose to the occasion. Such faith was what the Lord Jesus sought. Without actually seeing the miracle, the man believed.

"Thy son liveth." The Lord spoke these words around the seventh hour (John 4:52-53), or 1 PM. The man went his way, but apparently took his time. How relieved he would have been from the words of Christ, and his belief in the Master was so great that he didn't rush home to see if it was fulfilled. He believed that his son was getting better and he believed that the fever was leaving him. Thus, instead of the intense dash which he had done earlier in the day, he went at a more moderate pace. As a result, *the next day* his servants found him still on the road:

> "And as he was now going down, his servants met him, and told him, saying, Thy son liveth. Then enquired he of them the hour when he began to amend. And they said unto him, Yesterday at the seventh hour the fever left him." John 4:51-52

The man had pleaded with Christ and the miracle had been performed the day prior. It took the nobleman until the next day to complete his journey. He had made his request known to Christ and the peace of God was now keeping his heart and his mind.

But this peace was very different than the emotion which had filled his heart—and his house—just the day before. Just imagine the scene that had taken place in

Healing the Nobleman's Son

this man's house! The son was deathly ill, the mother would likely weeping beside his bedside, possibly even holding his weakened hand. Suddenly, in the seventh hour of the day, something unbelievable happened. The mother felt strength in her little boy's hand again! His fingers clasped around her's. She looked up—he was looking at her, smiling—as though he had never been sick!

Imagine the expression on her face! What had happened? How did this happen? When exactly did it happen? Quickly she had the servants document that it was the seventh hour when the fever left him and then she sent them off to find her husband. He didn't need to find the healer any longer—their son was well!

The servants were sent down the path to Cana to find the nobleman. When they saw him in the distance, they would have wondered why he was walking back alone— perhaps he was not able to find the healer. He apparently was walking home slowly, maybe overcome with sadness. Quickly they rushed up to him and gave him the news, "Thy son liveth!"

Imagine the surprise of the nobleman when this story was related to him! Imagine the joy! Imagine how this miracle would have fortified his faith. When he saw the servants, he asked them "the hour when he *began to amend*." Yet notice their response! "Yesterday at the seventh hour *the fever left him*." The fever left him! The man was expecting that his son would begin to amend, or slowly get better from his sickness—but this was not the type of cure brought about by the Lord Jesus. The fever completely left him. Immediately the son was back to his normal health and the disease was gone. Such was the power of God's Son.

> "So the father knew that it was at the same hour, in the which Jesus said unto him, Thy son liveth: and himself believed, and his whole house." John 4:53

Not only was the cure complete and entire, but it took place at the exact time that Christ had spoken the words. The nobleman was in awe of the man from Nazareth—his faith was confirmed and strengthened. The record simply says "and himself believed." The original faith which he placed in Christ's words had been validated and from that faith grew actions which brought the words of Christ to the rest of his household. The nobleman came home to his family and shared the news of everything that had happened and everything which Christ had said to him. As a result of what they had been told, his family believed as well.

There was one household in Capernaum which would never be the same again. They had come face to face with the Master, had felt the power of his words, and had been changed forever.

The Parable

The story of the nobleman is a moving testimony to the power of faith and the love of Christ towards those who seek to believe in his Word. Yet as with all of these pictures which John presents, there is more to them than just the surface story. There certainly are valuable lessons which come from the story, such as the power of true faith, but there is a parable beneath the story which is not to be missed.

Healing the Nobleman's Son
From the Jews to the Gentiles

When looking at the parable of the nobleman, one must first note the immediate context of the miracle. Jesus had left Judaea because of the Jews. After leaving Judaea, he went to the Samaritans.

> "He left Judaea, and departed again into Galilee. And he must needs go through Samaria." John 4:3-4

Because of opposition from the Jewish rulers, Christ left and turned to the Gentiles. In the parable, this perhaps matches up with the rejection of Christ by the Jews in the first century and beyond, and the acceptance of Christ by the Gentiles. As the Lord Jesus said in the parable of the vineyard:

> "Jesus saith unto them, Did ye never read in the scriptures, The stone which the builders rejected, the same is become the head of the corner: this is the Lord's doing, and it is marvelous in our eyes? Therefore say I unto you, <u>The kingdom of God shall be taken from you, and given to a nation bringing forth the fruits thereof.</u>" Matthew 21:42-43

Because the Jews rejected their Messiah, an opportunity was opened for the Gentiles to come into the hope of Israel. They would be able to take part in Israel's inheritance (Acts 20:32; Ephesians 2:12). This is exactly what the parable was showing in the beginning of John 4. The Jews had failed to recognize the true mission and purpose of Christ—they followed him simply because of the miracles, and so the Master departed from them. The group of people to whom he turned was the

Gentiles. This understanding of the context is supported by the next few verses:

> "Then cometh he to a city of Samaria, which is called Sychar, near to the parcel of ground that Jacob gave to his son Joseph. Now Jacob's well was there. Jesus therefore, being wearied with his journey, sat thus on the well: and it was about the sixth hour." John 4:5-6

After John told his readers about Jesus leaving Judaea and going to Samaria, he purposefully wrote that the Lord went to a place which was originally *Jewish inheritance!* This was right next to the land which Jacob had given to Joseph! Thus, at this time, the Jewish inheritance was occupied by *Gentiles!* In the parable, John was showing that the Lord had left preaching to the Jews to turn to the Gentiles (cp. Acts 13:46). Then, the Gentiles were given a portion in the inheritance of the Jews. The time which the Master spent with the Samaritans is representative of the time in which the gospel went out to the Gentiles and they were given the opportunity of an inheritance among Israel. While the Jews rejected the message and for a time lost their inheritance, the Gentiles believed and were able to come into the hope.

John really wanted to emphasize this point to his readers. Throughout his gospel he sought to show the belief of the Gentiles and the unbelief of the Jews. Thus, notice the similarities between what was said to the Samaritan woman in John 4 and what was spoken to the Jews in John 6—but also notice where the two conversations diverge.

Healing the Nobleman's Son

- The Lord offered to give something divine to his listeners:

    To the Samaritan woman:

    "Jesus answered and said unto her, If thou knewest the gift of God, and who it is that saith to thee, Give me to drink; thou wouldest have asked of him, and he would have given thee living water." John 4:10

    To the Jews:

    "Then Jesus said unto them, Verily, verily, I say unto you, Moses gave you not that bread from heaven; but my Father giveth you the true bread from heaven." John 6:32

- He connected his gift with eternal life:

    To the Samaritan woman:

    "Jesus answered and said unto her, Whosoever drinketh of this water shall thirst again: but whosoever drinketh of the water that I shall give him shall never thirst; but the water that I shall give him shall be in him a well of water <u>springing up into everlasting life</u>." John 4:13-14

    To the Jews:

    "For the bread of God is he which cometh down from heaven, and <u>giveth life unto the world</u>." John 6:33

- Both parties desired of the Lord that he would give them that of which he spoke:

The Samaritan woman:

"The woman saith unto him, Sir, give me this water, that I thirst not, neither come hither to draw." John 4:15

The Jews:

"Then said they unto him, Lord, evermore give us this bread." John 6:34

- Christ expressed his Messiahship:

To the Samaritan woman:

"The woman saith unto him, I know that Messias cometh, which is called Christ: when he is come, he will tell us all things. Jesus saith unto her, I that speak unto thee am he." John 4:25-26

To the Jews:

"And Jesus said unto them, I am the bread of life: he that cometh to me shall never hunger; and he that believeth on me shall never thirst...for I came down from heaven, not to do mine own will, but the will of him that sent me." John 6:35, 38

- Yet the Gentiles accepted the gift and for the time being, the Jews rejected it:

The Samaritan woman:

"Come, see a man, which told me all things that ever I did: is not this the Christ?" John 4:29

Healing the Nobleman's Son

The Jews:

> "From that time many of his disciples went back, and walked no more with him." John 6:66

The circumstances were similar, yet the reactions were completely different. This is what John was seeking to show with the story of the Samaritan woman. While the Jews had rejected the Lord Jesus Christ and had refused the gift of God, the Gentiles had accepted it. They believed.

> "So when the Samaritans were come unto him, they besought him that he would tarry with them: and he abode there two days. And many more believed because of his own word; and said unto the woman, Now we believe, not because of thy saying: for we have heard him ourselves, and know that this is indeed the Christ, the Savior of the world." John 4:40-42

The Gentiles had come to believe in Christ. This is the context of the miracle. After this, Jesus departed from the Gentiles and turned back to the Jews. It is at that point in the narrative that the nobleman entered into the story.

Connections to Israel

The nobleman and his son are together representative of Israel. This connection can be established from the comment made to the man by the Lord Jesus:

> "Then said Jesus unto him, Except ye see signs and wonders, ye will not believe." John 4:48

As mentioned earlier, this was what the Jews were constantly demanding of Christ! Over and over throughout the gospels they came to him asking him to show them a sign to prove that he was the Messiah. This was not so with the Gentiles, but with the Jews it came up repeatedly. Here are a few examples:

> "Then certain of the scribes and of the Pharisees answered, saying, Master, we would see a sign from thee." Matthew 12:38

The Lord Jesus had just responded to the Pharisees' latest attack—they claimed that he cast out demons by Beelzebub. He had explained the poor reasoning behind this, brought up the consequences of blaspheming the Holy Spirit, and then told them that they would have to give account at the judgment for every idle word which they had spoken. This was quite an intense and powerful answer to their accusation! Their poor response to him was that they needed to see a sign. Again, the idea of the sign comes up just a few chapters later in Matthew:

> "The Pharisees also with the Sadducees came, and tempting desired him that he would shew them a sign from heaven." Matthew 16:1

It was the same type of thing. The Jews were constantly seeking for the Lord to perform some type of miracle—yet he had just performed one right before their appeal! Just at the end of Matthew 15, the Lord Jesus fed the four thousand with seven loaves and a few fish. However, this either escaped the knowledge of the Jewish rulers or it wasn't enough for them. Still they

Healing the Nobleman's Son

insisted that he show them a sign. Once more, the same thing happened when Christ cleansed the temple:

> "Then answered the Jews and said unto him, What sign shewest thou unto us, seeing that thou doest these things?" John 2:18

It was the same line—"shew us a sign!" Here, Jesus had just cleansed the temple and the Jewish rulers demanded a sign of his authority. Over and over they pestered the Lord for a sign of his Messiahship. Yet there would be no sign given to them.

When the Lord said "Except ye see signs and wonders, ye will not believe" to the nobleman, he connected the man to Israel. The nobleman represents the Jews! However, not only does the nobleman represent the Jews, but his son does as well. Scripturally, Israel is referred to as God's "son."

> "And thou shalt say unto Pharaoh, Thus saith the LORD, Israel is my son, even my firstborn." Exodus 4:22

Israel is called God's firstborn son. Once more, the book of Hosea says the same thing:

> "When Israel was a child, then I loved him, and called my son out of Egypt." Hosea 11:1

Yahweh called His son out of Egypt. He saved Israel from the hand of the Egyptians. Israel is God's son. Thus, the son of the nobleman is also representative of Israel. The two of them together combine to give a fuller picture of the nation as a whole. Just like the nobleman's son, in the parable, Israel is deathly sick and they have come to Christ for healing. Their sickness is a fever (John 4:52)—which was one of the curses which God had promised if they were disobedient:

> "The LORD shall smite thee with a consumption, <u>and with a fever</u>, and with an inflammation, and with an extreme burning, and with the sword, and with blasting, and with mildew; and they shall pursue thee until thou perish." Deuteronomy 28:22

In the Septuagint translation, this is the same Greek word that is used in John 4. One of the curses which would come upon Israel if they left Yahweh was a "fever." This was exactly what was plaguing the young son of the nobleman. The nobleman shows a picture of an Israel which is finally willing to come to Christ for healing. They have been disobedient and forsaken their Maker, so God has punished them—just as He promised He would in Deuteronomy. Eventually, this punishment has become so terrible and so inhibiting that they are at the point of death.

Amazingly, in order to be healed, they come to the Lord Jesus Christ—but they have to prove that they have changed. They have to prove that they are not simply looking for him to perform great signs and wonders just as they have wanted in the past. They have to prove that they have faith.

Thus, just as the nobleman had to prove his faith by believing in the words of Christ, though he saw no miracle, so will Israel. They will have to come to Christ in faith, believing in his words. Only then will healing come.

Healing the Nobleman's Son

Why a Nobleman?

Yet why is Israel represented as royalty? Why did John specifically record that it was a "nobleman" who came to Christ? The reason is that "Israel" means "prince with God." Israel *is* royalty! A "nobleman" is an apt description of God's special people. But the connection goes even further. Though Israel was supposed to be a prince with God, they did not act or think as though they occupied that lofty position. By rejecting the Lord Jesus Christ, Israel rejected God as their king. Instead of ruling with Yahweh and having Him as their king, since the time of Christ, Israel has submitted themselves to the rulership and thinking of the world:

> "But they cried out, Away with him, away with him, crucify him. Pilate saith unto them, shall I crucify your King? The chief priests answered, <u>We have no king but Caesar.</u>" John 19:15

The Jews rejected God as their king and turned to a Gentile power. Israel is still a "prince with God," and the Jews are still God's special people, but instead of living up to their name, they submitted themselves to the reign of Caesar. So it was with this man—he was a special man, a ruler, just as Israel—but it is highly likely that as a ruler in Israel, he was an officer in Herod's court, which was located at Capernaum. He worked under the rulership of a Gentile. This man shows a picture of an Israel which has submitted to the power of the world ever since rejecting Christ. They are still a special and a royal people to God, yet their allegiance is questionable—however, soon things are about to change. Just as the nobleman did, Israel will humble themselves and fall before Christ.

Gentile Times

The story of the nobleman and his son comes just after the story of the faith of the Samaritans. As mentioned earlier, the story of the Samaritans is representative of the faith of the Gentiles and their opportunity to come into the hope of Israel. This time of their faith and opportunity is styled by the Lord Jesus Christ as "the times of the Gentiles."

> "And they shall fall by the edge of the sword, and shall be led away captive into all nations: and Jerusalem shall be trodden down of the Gentiles, until the times of the Gentiles be fulfilled." Luke 21:24

Once the "times of the Gentiles" have been fulfilled, then Jerusalem will be saved! They will be healed! This time of faith and true healing will be brought about at the second coming of Christ (Zechariah 12:9-10). The Lord Jesus and his saints will appear to save them at the battle of Armageddon, and though the Jews will learn to follow the Lord *in faith*. This is why John emphasized that this was the *second* sign which Jesus performed and that it was connected to the first sign.

> "So Jesus came again into Cana of Galilee, where he made the water wine. And there was a certain nobleman, whose son was sick at Capernaum." John 4:46

John specifically wanted to point out to the reader that this miracle took place in the exact same town where the

Healing the Nobleman's Son

water into wine happened. He purposefully connected the two miracles. Again, at the end of the sign:

> "This is again <u>the second miracle</u> that Jesus did, when he was come out of Judaea into Galilee." John 4:54

Twice John sought to show that this miracle was tied to the first miracle of the water into wine. This was done because the apostle was trying to get the reader to see in the signs the *first* and *second* comings of Christ! John didn't number any of the other signs which Jesus performed. Only the first and the second—which in this parable represent the first and the second coming of the Lord.

At his first coming, the Lord Jesus Christ brought new wine, which went all throughout the world and brought life and an opportunity to be in the Kingdom of God. In the meantime, the gospel was taken to the Gentiles and they were given an opportunity to enter into the inheritance. Finally, at his second coming, he will bring life to the Jews. They will believe upon him in true faith and they will be saved.

This sign is representative of the second coming of Christ, which takes place after the times of the Gentiles have been fulfilled. It is the time of Israel's healing. In the record, this all took place after Christ had been "two days" with the Gentiles.

> "So when the Samaritans were come unto him, they besought him that he would tarry with them: and he abode there <u>two days</u>...Now after <u>two days</u> he departed thence, and went into Galilee." John 4:40, 43

It's not at all an accident that Scripture records and emphasizes the "two days." Both of these days show the two thousand years in which the hope of Israel would be available to the Gentiles. At the same time, these days are perhaps an allusion back to the book of Hosea, where the healing of Israel was predicted after "two days."

> "Come, and let us return unto the LORD: for he hath torn, and he will heal us; he hath smitten, and he will bind us up. <u>After two days</u> will he revive us: in the third day he will raise us up, and we shall live in his sight." Hosea 6:1-2

Jesus stayed for two days with the Gentiles and on the third day he went to Galilee. It was on the third day that the son was revived. After two thousand years of the gospel being preached to the Gentiles, the hope will once again be accepted by the Jews. They will be healed in the seventh hour—or the seventh millennium.

Lesson

The parable of the nobleman's son is a beautiful picture of the redemption of God's people at the second coming of Christ. Israel, who is living in death, will be healed. They will come to Christ in faith. They will recognize their position and they will humbly fall before the Master. This is an important distinction to make—Israel is the one that comes to Christ. During the battle of Armageddon, they will turn to Yahweh *first*, before they are saved:

Healing the Nobleman's Son

> "Let the priests, the ministers of the LORD, weep between the porch and the altar, and let them say, Spare thy people, O LORD, and give not thine heritage to reproach, that the heathen should rule over them: wherefore should they say among the people, Where is their God?" Joel 2:17-18

When the Jews have been trodden down by the northern invader, they will turn to God. They will finally recognize their need. They will know that they cannot do it on their own, they will see that they are in desperate need of healing, and they will pray. As it was said in Hosea, "Come, and let us return unto the LORD." Israel will have to humble themselves and come to Yahweh in faith. Only then will they be brought from death to life.

So it is with us. In looking at this sign and in looking at this parable, let us not forget that we too have been changed by the Lord.

> "And you hath he quickened, <u>who were dead in trespasses and sins</u>; wherein time past ye walked according to the course of this world, according to the prince of the power of the air, the spirit that now worketh in the children of disobedience..." Ephesians 2:1-2

Before being healed by Christ, we were dying. We were on the path to the grave, forever. But by His grace, God has given each of us an opportunity for life. He offers it to everyone of us. It doesn't come in some type of successful life, as the world would define it. It doesn't come in worldly fame. It is attained by coming to the Lord Jesus Christ. It is attained by falling at his feet and beseeching him that he might heal us of our sin. The method of healing—faithful obedience to Christ—is not what one would typically think would bring salvation, yet just like Israel and just like the nobleman, we come away from that meeting with the Lord in faith, believing that he will do what he has said.

Our faith isn't built upon a miracle which we have seen. Our faith isn't dependent upon seeing someone given eternal life. Christ has made the promise, and we believe it. May we continue to hold on to this belief and live in it throughout the rest of our lives—knowing that he who endures to the end, the same shall be saved.

Chapter 3
The Invalid

The story of the nobleman was a story about the healing of the Jews. Eventually, they will recognize their need to turn back to Yahweh and they will repent—in doing so, they will humbly be brought to the Lord Jesus Christ. With his mighty power, he will heal them. It's a picture of the Jews faithfully turning to Christ to receive life—however, it is a picture which is delayed. The full fulfillment of this parable does not yet occur until the times of the Gentiles have ended and until the Master has come again.

Before this healing of the Jews will take place and before the Kingdom age, much has happened with the Hebrew people. Through the hardness of their hearts, they turned from the One who sought to save them—and it is that tragic message which this sign tells. It tells the story of the Jews at the time of Christ and their reaction to their Messiah. The story began when the Master entered Jerusalem...

A Feast of the Jews

> "After this there was a feast of the Jews; and Jesus went up to Jerusalem." John 5:1

The narrative began in Jerusalem, at the time of a feast. This feast was specifically called a feast "of the Jews." This term, "the Jews," is a phrase which was specifically used by John to denote those Jews who were wrapped

Glimpses of the Master

up in their traditions and rituals. Constantly throughout his book he used it in this way. Here are some examples:

- In John 2, the Master came to the temple and overturned the tables of the moneychangers. After this, a group of people angrily come to the Lord, demanding to know why he believed that he could do such a thing:

"Then answered <u>the Jews</u> and said unto him, What sign shewest thou unto us, seeing that thou doest these things?" John 2:18

John didn't say that the Sadducees came to the Lord, or that the priests came to him. Instead, he specifically referred to these people as "the Jews." This was John's special term for the people who were entrenched in their rituals.

- Just one chapter later, John the Baptist's disciples began to dispute with a group of people about the ritual of purifying. Again, the group which disagreed with them was called "the Jews":

"Then there arose a question between some of John's disciples and <u>the Jews</u> about purifying." John 3:25

Standing against the disciples of John the Baptist were "the Jews."

- Even in the present story about the invalid, the people who rebuked healed man for carrying his mat on the Sabbath were called "the Jews":

The Invalid

> "The Jews therefore said unto him that was cured, It is the sabbath day: it is not lawful for thee to carry thy bed." John 5:10

John consistently used this term to speak about the specific group of Jewish people who were stuck in the traditions of men.

This story opens with a "feast of the Jews." Thus, with a new understanding of John's term, it can be seen that this was a feast which had become burdened with the rituals and commands of the rulers of the day. It had lost its true significance. It was a feast of *the Jews*. To make the meaning even stronger, notice the way that the law of Moses actually referred to the feasts:

> "Speak unto the children of Israel, and say unto them, Concerning the feasts of the LORD, which he shall proclaim to be holy convocations, even these are my feasts." Leviticus 23:2

The feasts were originally called feasts of Yahweh! They were *His feasts*! Again, the book of Ezra refers to the feasts in the same way:

> "And afterward offered the continual burnt offering, both of the new moons, and of all the set feasts of the LORD that were consecrated, and of every one that willing offered a freewill offering unto the LORD." Ezra 3:5

When God commanded Moses to initiate the set feasts throughout the year, they were created as feasts in which the people would come to worship Yahweh Himself. They were a gift and a service to Him—they were a special time for the people to focus their minds upon

His goodness and upon their thankfulness for His provision. They were the "feasts of the LORD." But, by the time that Christ came to the Jewish people, the law of Moses had become so corrupted, that the feasts were no longer "feasts of the LORD." Instead, they were "feasts of the Jews"—those people who were led by their traditions. Essentially, the feasts had lost their purpose—they had become old wine.

John opened his chapter with this powerful phrase, showing his readers the way in which the Jews had fallen from the principles of the law. This beginning verse tends to set the theme for the rest of the chapter and the rest of the sign. All throughout this chapter, there is a focus on the defunct ceremonies and corruption of the religious people at that time.

The Lord's Discourse

This theme continues through the story of the healing of the invalid man, and is also shown in the reaction of the Jews to Christ's miracle:

> "And therefore did the Jews persecute Jesus, and sought to slay him, because he had done these things on the sabbath day." John 5:16

This was the first time in which the Jews of the day wanted to kill Christ. They had strayed so far from God's principles that they found themselves fighting against His Son, and upholding their misunderstandings rather than God's Truth. This animosity towards Christ was not something which went away quickly. The hatred that resulted from this miracle continued to follow the

The Invalid

Lord for more than a year. About a year and a half after healing the invalid, the Jews were still trying to kill him:

> "Did not Moses give you the law, and yet none of you keepeth the law? <u>Why go ye about to kill me?</u> The people answered and said, Thou hast a devil: who goeth about to kill thee? Jesus answered and said unto them, I have done one work, and ye all marvel. Moses therefore gave unto you circumcision; (not because it is of Moses, but of the fathers;) and ye on the sabbath day circumcise a man. If a man on the sabbath day receive circumcision, that the law of Moses should not be broken; <u>are ye angry at me, because I have made a man every whit whole on the sabbath day?</u>" John 7:19-23

Even at the feast of tabernacles, over a year and a half later, the Jews still wanted to kill Christ for his act of healing upon this man! Again, the chapter is bringing out the way that the religious rulers of the day had zealously held close to their teachings, and subsequently fell from the teaching of God.

This theme even flows throughout the ensuing discourse by the Lord Jesus. Just after the miraculous healing of the lame man, Christ (with John's narration) gave a speech which was riddled with criticism for the Jewish corruption of the law. Throughout this discourse, the Master turned to many of the commandments of the law, and then showed that the Jews had broken that commandment. Over and over he went through their law, showing that they had entirely flouted that which they claimed to love. He began with the command about the Sabbath.

- Remember the Sabbath day and keep it holy (Exodus 20:8-10)

"But Jesus answered them, My Father worketh hitherto, and I work." John 5:17

Christ had healed on a Sabbath, and the religious rulers were full of fury. In their minds, the Sabbath was not at all a day to be doings such things—but the Lord explained to them otherwise. Throughout time, God had worked on the sabbath—therefore, he would work as well. The sabbath was a day to do the works of God, to set aside their own fancies and their own desires, and to follow Yahweh. The religious rulers had completely missed the principle. It wasn't about preventing people from carrying their mat! Yet their violation of the law wasn't simply in their violation of the sabbath. John went on to show even more ways that the Jews had broken God's commands.

- Thou shalt not kill (Exodus 20:13)

"Therefore the Jews sought the more to kill him, because he not only had broken the sabbath, but said also that God was his Father, making himself equal with God." John 5:18

Though they had been commanded not to kill, the Jews now set about to kill a righteous man. Yet there was more—the Master was not finished.

- Honor thy Father and mother (Exodus 20:12)

"That all men should honor the Son, even as they honor the Father. He that honoreth not the Son

The Invalid

honoreth not the Father which hath sent him." John 5:23

If they did not honor the Son, then they did not honor the Father. Truly, they wanted to kill the Son—meaning that they were in no way honoring the Father. But there was still a greater command which they had broken. Not only had their traditions led them to breaking the ten commandments—they had also broken the greatest commandment.

- The greatest commandment (Deuteronomy 6:5)

"But I know you, that ye have not the love of God in you." John 5:42

Near the end of his speech, the Lord took his hearers to the "greatest" commandment and told them that they had even broken that—"thou shalt love the LORD thy God." The religious leaders had missed the point. In their feverish devotion to their doctrines, they had missed the weightier matters of the law. They forgot to love Yahweh their God. They forgot to devote all of their being to Him. Their negligence in these things actually led to them violating the very law which they loved, and being condemned by Moses—the man whom they thought they followed. Instead, they were nothing like him—and the Master did not ignore the opportunity to make them aware of this.

"And the Father himself, which hath sent me, hath borne witness of me. <u>Ye have neither heard his voice at any time, nor seen his shape.</u>" John 5:37

These men had never heard the voice of God and they had never seen His shape. They had never had that strong and living connection with God—but there was someone who had. Moses had—Moses *had* heard His voice and *had* seen His shape. Moses was a prophet unlike any other. He was the prophet to whom God spoke, and he was the prophet with whom God worked face to face.

> "My servant Moses is not so, who is faithful in all mine house. <u>With him will I speak mouth to mouth</u>, even apparently, and not in dark speeches; and <u>the similitude of the LORD shall he behold</u>: wherefore then were ye not afraid to speak against my servant Moses?" Numbers 12:7-8

Moses saw the shape of the LORD and he heard His voice, unlike the Jewish rulers of the day! The book of Deuteronomy even says that God knew Moses face to face (Deuteronomy 34:10)! These men claimed to be Moses' disciples, yet they were nothing like him. They did not follow in his steps and they broke his commandments by their traditions. They did not know what Moses truly commanded, and as a result they didn't realize that the things the Lord Jesus did were a direct fulfillment of what Moses had prophesied when he spoke of the "Prophet" who would come. Thus, the Lord continued to focus on showing them their inconsistency. They were nothing like Moses—but the situation was even more desperate. Not only were they nothing like him, but they were actually aligned against him! Their doctrines and their rituals had brought them to the point where they were *standing against* Moses, the one whom they claimed to love.

> "Do not think that I will accuse you to the Father: there is one that accuseth you, even Moses, in whom ye trust. For had ye believed Moses, ye would have

The Invalid

believed me: for he wrote of me. But if ye believe
not his writings, how shall ye believe my words?"
John 5:45-47

The very one whom they claimed to love actually
condemned them. They had broken multiple
commandments, they had turned the feasts of God into
a feast to themselves, and they sought to kill the Son of
God. All together, this inept worship and sad reaction to
Christ is the main focus of this chapter.

Accordingly, the parable shows the same theme—but
first, the story itself must be examined. As the story
unfolds, it will be seen how well its details fit with the
context.

The Story

> "After this there was a feast of the Jews; and Jesus
> went up to Jerusalem. Now there is at Jerusalem by
> the sheep market a pool, which is called in the
> Hebrew tongue Bethesda, having five porches. In
> these lay a great multitude of impotent folk, of
> blind, halt, withered, waiting for the moving of the
> water. For an angel went down at a certain season
> into the pool, and troubled the water: whosoever
> then first after the troubling of the water stepped in
> was made whole of whatsoever disease he had."
> John 5:1-4

Jesus had previously been preaching in Galilee, but he
changed his course and chose to go down to Jerusalem,
to a specific pool there—called the pool of Bethesda.
This pool was believed to have special healing
qualities—it was periodically touched by an angel, and

just after that touch occurred, whoever was the first person to get into the pool would be healed of their infirmities. This angelic intervention may have been just a superstition among the people—many newer translations indicate that in a footnote of some sort. Nevertheless, the validity of this phrase doesn't strongly affect the story either way, and will not be dealt examined here. Suffice it to say that the manuscript of the King James version is followed here because it gives the lame man's comment a fuller context (John 5:7).

This pool was a place which was surrounded with the sick and diseased. However, Christ didn't go there to heal everyone. He had a specific purpose in mind.

Thirty Eight Years

> "And a certain man was there, which had an infirmity thirty and eight years." John 5:5

There was a man at the pool who had been crippled for thirty eight years. Year after year he had come to the pool and had never been healed. But things were about to change.

> "When Jesus saw him lie, and knew that he had been now a long time in that case, he saith unto him, Wilt thou be made whole?" John 5:6

The shadow of the Master passed over this man. "Do you want to be made well?" It seems almost a strange question to ask someone who has been sick for thirty eight years—yet it wasn't. The response of the lame man gives a powerful insight into the actual meaning of the Lord's question:

The Invalid

> "The impotent man answered him, Sir, I have no man, when the water is troubled, to put me into the pool: but while I am coming, another steppeth down before me." John 5:7

The man didn't automatically say "Yes I do!" or "Of course!" Rather, it's almost as though his response was a defense—"I don't have anyone to help me. When the angel comes down, someone else always gets to the water first." He made an excuse for why he hadn't already been healed. He tried to explain how it was possible that he had come to that pool for thirty eight years and had not been made whole—a very strange response if the Lord's question had merely been a simple, "Would you like to feel better?"

But there may be a little bit more to the story. Perhaps this answer was given because there was more behind the Lord's question than it would initially appear. The Lord wasn't asking a question out of sympathy. He had specifically come to this man because he had a purpose to show with him. Christ's question was much more pointed—a question which made the lame man put up his defenses and give an excuse; something more like "how could you have come to this pool for thirty eight years and still be an invalid? Why have you not been healed? Do you *really* want to be made well?"

When the Lord's question is understood in this way, the answer fits perfectly. "Sir, I have no man, when the water is troubled, to put me into the pool: but while I am coming, another steppeth down before me."

Try to imagine the scene. Somehow this man had come to the pool each day for thirty eight years. It's doubtful that he stayed the night there—and even if he did, he at least would have had to move about in order to relieve himself. If he had the ability to move around a bit, then it's probable that he could have pushed himself into the water at least once in *thirty eight* years—surely there would have been at least *one opportunity*. On the other hand, if someone did typically help him to get to the pool each day, wouldn't they have been willing to stay a few days to help him slip into the water? Something seems a bit odd about this situation—thirty eight years is a long time to be in one place; how was it possible for this man to have been at this pool for *so long* and yet still be inform. Truly, did he want to be healed? Or perhaps, the life of a beggar was a little too easy for him; with healing came responsibility.

Thus, Christ looked into the heart of this man and asked "Do you *actually* want to be made whole?"

Take Up Thy Bed

After the invalid gave his feeble defense, Christ commanded him to rise:

> "Jesus saith unto him, Rise, take up thy bed, and walk. And immediately the man was made whole, and took up his bed, and walked: and on the same day was the sabbath." John 5:8

Immediately the man was healed and took up his bed. It would seem that despite his seemingly lethargic attitude, Christ healed him. All was glorious—but the Lord had healed on a Sabbath, and he had healed *deliberately* on the Sabbath. He could have chosen any other day to perform this miracle, yet he did it on the sabbath—

The Invalid

because the focus of this chapter is to show the complete failure of the Jewish traditions. The Master was about to come head to head with the Jews and their rituals.

The man picked up his bed and began walking—as he was doing this, he was sighted by the Jews.

> "The Jews therefore said unto him that was cured, It is the sabbath day: it is not lawful for thee to carry thy bed." John 5:10

Carrying a bed on the Sabbath was not something that was allowed; it was probably considered "bearing a burden." God had commanded rest; therefore, in the minds of the Jews, no one could carry *anything*. Sadly, the rulers completely missed the point of what this day of rest was supposed to teach. Forget about taking time to serve God, forget about thinking on Him—just make sure that you don't carry anything! It was a total misunderstanding of the principles of God. Nevertheless, the invalid answered them:

> "He answered them, He that made me whole, the same said unto me, Take up thy bed, and walk. Then asked they him, What man is that which said unto thee, Take up thy bed, and walk? And he that was healed wist not who it was: for Jesus had conveyed himself away, a multitude being in that place." John 5:11-13

It was an interesting response from the man. It seems characteristic with how he had been portrayed so far in the record. He deflected this wrath—"the man who healed me told me to." "Who healed you?" "I don't know." And that was it. What a contrast to the man healed a few chapters later—the man born blind! This invalid deflected the attention of the Jews and wanted to get away as soon as possible. As a contrast, the man born blind stood up to them and vouched for the name of Christ!

The man gave a response that seems to fit with what has been observed before. The Pharisees responded characteristically as well. They knew full well that the man had been healed—"he that made me whole." The words fell to the ground as soon as the man had said them. Never mind that a miracle had been performed, never mind that this man had been lame for thirty eight years and could finally jump about. The Sabbath had been broken, their traditions had been pushed aside—and this healer was worse than just the ordinary Sabbath breaker. He was a person who was going around and *telling* people to break the Sabbath! These views could start to spread! Their entire way of worshipping God was being undermined. Someone needed to be punished—and the man healed wanted to make sure that the someone wasn't him. Thus decided to head towards the temple:

> "Afterward Jesus findeth him in the temple, and said unto him, Behold, thou art made whole: sin no more, lest a worse thing come unto thee." John 5:14

A part of us longs to interpret the presence of this man in the temple as a good and faithful thing. Maybe he was there because he wanted to thank God for his new found health. Yet those thoughts are dispelled by the words spoken by the Lord. He was abrupt and to the point: "Sin no more, lest a worse thing come unto thee." Again, the Master's words give more insight into the story behind this man.

The Invalid

Jesus found him in the temple and didn't give him words of encouragement. Instead, he warned him. He wasn't friendly and congenial. He was blunt and stern. In fact, other translations add another dimension to Christ's words here:

> "After these things, Jesus findeth him, in the temple, and said unto him—See! thou hast become, well:— <u>No more, be committing sin</u>, lest, some worse thing, do thee befall." John 5:14 Rotherham

> "Later Jesus found him at the temple and said to him, "See, you are well again. <u>Stop sinning</u> or something worse may happen to you." John 5:14 NIV

The way that these translations put the words of the Lord, it sounds as though the man had been living in constant sin. "Stop sinning..." Perhaps this man had been living a life of sin—possibly a prolonged life of deceitful begging when he actually could have been healed. This man wasn't the type of person that was a picture of righteousness. Instead, he had been living in sin, and Christ warned that if he continued in that lifestyle, something even worse would happen to him. This is why Christ said "Do you want to be made well?" This is why the man never defended the one who healed him.

Nevertheless, if this was the man's character, then why did he eventually go to the temple? Perhaps his motive was slightly less noble than would initially be imagined. Perhaps, as would seem to fit with his personality, he didn't go to the temple to thank God, but rather to show the religious rulers that he actually was an obedient follower of their laws. Perhaps he was trying to win favor back with them. If such was the case, it would certainly fit with what he did next:

> "The man departed, and told the Jews that it was Jesus, which had made him whole." John 5:15

The man left the Lord in the temple and told the Jews that it was him who had healed him. Surely this was an act of betrayal! The Jews had come to him and upbraided him for carrying his mat. He pushed the blame off to the one who had made him whole. They then asked who it was who healed him so that they could punish that person. Instead of being grateful to Christ, this man effectively turned him in to the authorities! He had to know that they weren't going to be happy with the Lord for what he had done! Again, contrast this to the man born blind:

> "Jesus heard that they had cast him out; and when he had found him, he said unto him, Dost thou believe on the Son of God? He answered and said, Who is he, Lord, that I might believe on him? And Jesus said unto him, Thou hast both seen him, and it is he that talketh with thee. And he said, Lord, I believe, and he worshipped him." John 9:35-38

The man born blind believed and worshipped Christ. The lame man didn't believe and didn't worship Christ. Instead, he was upbraided by the Lord and turned him in to the Jews. What a contrast! Again, another helpful comparison is with another lame man who was healed by Peter and John.

> "Then Peter said, Silver and gold have I none; but such as I have give I thee: In the name of Jesus

The Invalid

Christ of Nazareth rise up and walk. And he took him by the right hand, and lifted him up: and immediately his feet and ankle bones received strength. And he leaping up stood, and walked, and entered with them into the temple, walking, and leaping, and praising God." Acts 3:6-8

After this man was healed, he entered into the temple and was walking and leaping and praising God! His was an attitude of pure thanks and joy. Yet John never recorded what the man from the pool of Bethesda did in the temple. Scripture never says that he praised God. It never says anything about what he did—which is a huge contrast to every other time someone went to the temple to worship God—Scripture *always* says that they were there praising Him (cp. Luke 2:37, Luke 24:53, John 7:14, John 8:2, Acts 2:46). And there is nothing written about this man glorifying God in *any* way. In fact, the Lord never said anything positive or encouraging to him throughout the whole narrative. The Master's words to him make up three brief sentences:

- "Wilt thou be made whole?"
- "Rise, take up thy bed and walk."
- "Behold, thou art made whole: sin no more, lest a worse thing come upon thee."

The words of the Master don't seem to convey a positive attitude. They are succinct and are devoid of any encourageent. All of these things come together to show that there was something not quite right about this man. Therefore, why did Christ go specifically to the pool of Bethesda and heal only him? And why did he disappear from the pool so quickly after this man was made well?

This whole miracle—just as the others—burns with the idea that there is something more beneath it. Why did Christ heal this man who was steeped in his sinful life, and who didn't really want to be healed in the first place? What was the idea behind this?

The answer lies in the fact that he was showing a parable—and in this parable, he reinforced the lesson of the chapter—the unwillingness of the Jews to leave their traditions and live according to God's principles.

The Parable

In writing the parable, the apostle immediately created little connections between the lame man and the Jewish people. Just note some of these:

The Sheep Gate

John specifically told his readers that the man spent his time at the sheep market, or the sheep gate.

> "Now there is at Jerusalem <u>by the sheep market</u> a pool, which is called in the Hebrew tongue Bethesda, having five porches." John 5:2

Why did John deem it necessary to tell his readers that the pool where the man spent all of his time was next to the sheep gate? Perhaps it was just a point of identification—but at the same time, perhaps John was trying to create an echo for his readers back to the Old Testament. Throughout the Old Testament, God referred to His people (the Jews) as His sheep:

The Invalid

> "My people hath been lost sheep: their shepherds have caused them to go astray, they have turned them away on the mountains: they have gone from mountain to hill, they have forgotten their restingplace." Jeremiah 50:6

In the prophets, Israel is described as lost sheep. Their leaders were directing them to the wrong places. This picture is painted in even more detail in Ezekiel.

> "Son of man, prophesy against the shepherds of Israel, prophesy, and say unto them, Thus saith the Lord GOD unto the shepherds; Woe be to the shepherds of Israel that do feed themselves! should not the shepherds feed the flocks? Ye eat the fat, and ye clothe you with the wool, ye kill them that are fed: but ye feed not the flock. The diseased have ye not strengthened, neither have ye healed that which was sick, neither have ye bound up that which was broken, neither have ye brought again that which was driven away, neither have ye sought that which was lost, but with force and with cruelty have ye ruled them." Ezekiel 34:2-4

God's people had been oppressed by their shepherds. Instead of leading them toward Yahweh, their shepherds actually took them away from Him and served themselves with their position! They did not heal the sick, they did not help the poor—because of them, their people were invalids! Just like this man! This man represents the average Jewish people—those who had been oppressed and broken by the zealous shepherds. He was maimed, sitting near the gate for the sheep, and at a specific pool called Bethesda.

Bethzatha

Bethesda means "house of mercy," yet mercy does not seem to fit very well with the theme of this chapter. However, it's possible that there may be an alternate reading for the name of this pool. A few versions actually read "Bethzatha" instead of "Bethesda."

> "Now there is in Jerusalem by the Sheep Gate a pool, in Hebrew called Bethzatha, which has five porticoes." John 5:2 RSV

> "Now there is in Jerusalem, at the Sheep-gate, a pool, which is called in Hebrew Bethzatha,—having, five porches." John 5:2 Rotherham

Both the NKJV and the NIV have "Bethzatha" in their footnotes. This begins to make the parable a bit more interesting, because it fits perfectly with the meaning of the sheep gate. Rather than "house of mercy," "Bethzatha" means "house of olives"—and throughout the Word of God, the olive tree is connected to Israel (Isaiah 17:6; Romans 11:17). Again, John was hinting that this man represents the Jewish people.

If the sheep gate and Bethzatha were not enough to connect this man to Israel, John gave another connection. The man had been lame for thirty eight years.

Thirty Eight Years

There is only one other place in Scripture where thirty eight years is mentioned. It's in reference to the children of Israel and their wilderness wanderings.

The Invalid

> "Now rise up, said I, and get you over the brook Zered. And we went over the brook Zered. And the space in which we came from Kadesh-barnea, until we were come over the brook Zered, was <u>thirty and eight years</u>; until all the generation of the men of war were wasted out from among the host, as the LORD sware unto them." Deuteronomy 2:13-14

It took Israel two years to move from Egypt to the Promised Land. From there, God cursed them for their disbelief and caused them to wander in the wilderness for forty years. Two of those years had already passed, therefore the actual time of the wilderness wanderings was thirty eight years. Israel wandered for thirty eight years in the wilderness—and notice what Moses said to them just after their thirty eight years of wandering was finished. He said, "Now rise up." Does that sound vaguely familiar? It's the same thing that the Lord Jesus said to the man—"Rise, take up thy bed, and walk."

The thirty eight years and the words of the Lord draw a clear parallel to the children of Israel who wasted away in the wilderness for thirty eight years—so this man was wasting away in his infirmity. However, the hand of healing was soon to reach out to him.

Healed

While the Lord was with the Jewish people, he asked them questions that made them uncomfortable—questions which clearly showed that their current way of life was wrong. This matches up with his question to the man—"Do you really want to be made well?" He asked them questions which made them think about contradictions that arose from their corrupted law. For many of them, his words had a slight healing affect, yet the words never truly made them whole. People followed him and learned from him, but soon after, they departed from him.

> "From that time many of his disciples went back, and walked no more with him." John 6:66

Again, just a few chapters later, John wrote of the way that the Jews were "healed" and then turned again to their old ways.

> "As he spake these words, <u>many believed on him</u>." John 8:30

Many believed on him! But, as he continued to speak, things quickly changed:

> "And because I tell you the truth, <u>ye believe me not</u>." John 8:45

Christ brought a measure of healing to Israel, but he never fully cured them—because they didn't really want to be healed. He brought them the warning, "sin no more, lest a worse thing befall thee." Yet unfortunately, just like this man, they turned back to their traditions and rituals—because many of them never really wanted true healing in the first place:

> "For this people's heart is waxed gross, and their ears are dull of hearing, and their eyes they have closed; lest at any time they should see with their eyes, and hear with their ears, and should understand with their heart, and should be converted, and I should heal them." Matthew 13:15

The Invalid

The Jews had closed their own eyes! They didn't want to be healed, just like the lame man. Thus, after Christ had brought a measure of healing to them, they went back to the Jewish authorities, again, like the invalid.

Sin No More

Nevertheless, just like with this man, the Master did not give up on them. He continued to go to Israel and to seek to cause them to repent, to proclaim to them, "Go, sin no more, lest a worse thing come upon thee!"

> "I tell you, Nay: but, except ye repent, ye shall all likewise perish." Luke 13:3

Repent. Change. Stop sinning—that was his message. Yet the people refused—and eventually, just like the lame man, they betrayed him. And so just as with this man, the warning given by Christ—"sin no more, lest a worse thing befall thee," would came true in a horrific way.

A Worse Thing

The tragedies that took place at AD 70, when Jerusalem was besieged by the Romans and the temple burnt to the ground were some of the most atrocious in history. Christ, in his Olivet prophecy described it as such.

> "<u>For then shall be great tribulation, such as was not since the beginning of the world to this time, no, nor ever shall be</u>. And except those days should be shorted, there should no flesh be saved: but for the

elect's sake those days shall be shortened." Matthew 24:21-22

The afflictions of AD 70 would be horrendous. A "worse thing" truly did come upon Israel, because they didn't repent. Josephus described the destruction in similar terms:

> "I shall therefore speak my mind here at once briefly:—<u>That neither did any other city ever suffer such miseries</u>, nor did any age ever breed a generation more fruitful in wickedness than this was, from the beginning of the world." Josephus; *The Wars of the Jews;* Book 5:10

Josephus was a Jewish general and a historian—a man who had been through war and knew the history of many wars. Yet as an eyewitness to the sufferings of Jerusalem, he said that he had never heard of a worse tragedy to come upon *any* city. The atrocities of AD 70 came about because of the failure of Israel to turn to their Messiah. They didn't want to change, they didn't want to give up their rituals. They were blinded and they wanted it so.

The Lesson

This really is the focus of this chapter in John. The Jews had so engrossed themselves in their traditions and practices, that they totally missed the principles and the lessons that God was trying to teach. It's not that the law was bad—the issue was the way that the people reacted to it! In fact, neither the Lord Jesus Christ nor the apostle Paul taught that the law was unrighteous—

The Invalid

Paul actually called it "good" (Romans 7:12; 1 Timothy 1:8)!

Instead, the issue was that the Jews tried to find salvation by the *works* of the law. They missed its principles. They were so caught up with what they thought was important, they missed the real purpose. As a result, the one whom they thought they followed actually ended up being the one who condemned them.

Let's keep this in mind.

Let's not be so blinded by what we think God wants that we are angry when we see His hand at work. Instead, let us fill our minds with the mind of God and with His Word. Let us read it every day and let us engulf ourselves in the Divine principles.

In doing so, we will begin to think like Christ. We will begin to be able to discern right from wrong, and will be able to apply Scriptural reasoning to situations before us.

The beautiful thing about all of this is that even though the specific Jews in Christ's day were never able to transform their minds in this way, and even though the successive generations were not able to either, God has never cast away his people. The term "Bethzatha," or "house of olives" reminiscent of Romans 11 and the olive tree of Israel:

> "I say then, Hath God cast away his people? God forbid...how much more shall these, which be the natural branches, be grafted into their own olive tree...And so all Israel shall be saved: as it is written, There shall come out of Sion the Deliverer, and shall

turn away ungodliness from Jacob." Romans 11:1, 24, 26

Unlike that man at the pool of Bethzatha, there will be a generation of Jewish people who look into the eyes of the Lord Jesus Christ, who look at his hands and at his side—and recognize that they have sinned. Yet instead of giving an excuse, like that man, they will repent and mourn for their blindness.

And they will be healed.

"And so all Israel shall be saved."

Chapter 4
Feeding the Five Thousand

There is one major difference between the feeding of the five thousand and the other major signs in John. Unlike the turning of the water into wine, the healing of the nobleman's son, and the healing of the man at the pool of Bethesda—which were all *solely* recorded by John—the feeding of the five thousand was remembered by all four gospel writers. There are four accounts to put together in order to get the full story. As this chapter seeks to piece together the whole picture of the feeding of the five thousand, it will draw from all four accounts. Some of them give details which are not recorded by any of the other writers. Then, when finding the the parable beneath the story, the details will be drawn exclusively from the gospel of John. When writing his account, John had a specific picture in mind which he was trying to teach with his parable; thus, he only recorded certain details and left out others.

As in the previous chapters, first will come the story. Then, after the picture has been presented, the parable will be examined.

John began the story by telling his readers that Jesus crossed over the sea of Galilee and was followed by a great multitude:

> "After these things Jesus went over the sea of Galilee, which is the sea of Tiberias. And a great multitude followed him, because they saw his

miracles which he did on them that were diseased."
John 6:1-2

The Lord crossed over Galilee and was followed by a great multitude. Unlike the other gospel writers, the apostle John never explained the reason for Jesus' crossing over the sea. Why did he take a boat instead of walking? Typically he walked almost everywhere that he went. The gospel of Mark helps to answer this question and provides the context of the feeding of the five thousand.

> "And the apostles gathered themselves together unto Jesus, and told him all things, both what they had done, and what they had taught. And he said unto them, Come ye yourselves apart into a desert place, and rest a while: for there were many coming and going, and they had no leisure so much as to eat."
> Mark 6:30-31

The disciples had just returned to Christ from their missionary campaign. They had been given the power of the Holy Spirit and had been commissioned to go from city to city preaching that the Kingdom of God was at hand (Matthew 10:7). This was their message. As they travelled throughout Israel, they had told the people that the Kingdom of God was near and would soon come into existence. At this time, immediately before the feeding of the five thousand, the disciples had just returned to the Lord from one of their first preaching campaigns. They came to him and told him all that had happened—all of the different miracles which they had been able to perform and all of the different responses which their message had received.

Feeding the Five Thousand

This was a time that the Lord Jesus would have wanted to spend alone with his disciples. They had been apart from him for a while, they needed his influence, and possibly he wanted to gently correct some of the things that they had done while away preaching. Unfortunately, their current location made this impossible. Mark said "they had no leisure so much as to eat." People were coming and going around them, possibly asking things of the Lord. He wanted to be alone with his disciples, and he wanted to discuss with them. Thus, the command was given that they should cross over sea:

> "Come ye yourselves apart into a desert place, and rest a while..."

It was time for rest. In addition to wanting to influence the thinking of the disciples and hear more about their journeys, it seems as though the Lord wanted the disciples to have some time to rejuvenate. Preaching is tiring and they needed to be rest. Some time alone with the Master would be perfect for what they needed.

Yet there was another reason for the departure of Christ and the disciples. Not only did Jesus want to have some private time with them to discuss their preaching, and not only were the disciples tired and worn from all of their travels—but Jesus himself was confronted with a sorrowful situation. John the Baptist had just been killed.

> "And he sent, and beheaded John in the prison. And his head was brought in a charger, and given to the damsel: and she brought it to her mother. And his disciples came, and took up the body, and buried it, and went and told Jesus. When Jesus heard of it, he departed thence by ship into a desert place apart: and

when the people had heard thereof, they follow him on foot out of the cities." Matthew 14:10-13

This must have been a tragic day for Jesus and his little band. At least two of Christ's disciples, John and Andrew, had originally been followers of John the Baptist. John was the one who originally brought them to Christ in John 1. John the Baptist was a kinsman of the Lord and probably a dear friend. His death would have completely confused the disciples—they were expecting the Kingdom of God to come immediately (Luke 19:11); it would have also been quite difficult for Christ since he had lost a close friend in the faith. Yet at the same time, the Lord Jesus hadn't just lost a friend—he had lost a forerunner. The job of John was to prepare the way for the Lord (Matthew 11:10) and to go before him (Luke 1:17).

John's death would have struck the Lord deeply. Here was the one who was to prepare the people for the work of the Messiah—and he had just been killed. John's work was over, and soon the Lord's would be too. In this situation, Christ would have sharply felt the nearness of his own death. John's death pointed forward to what would take place on Calvary—it foretold of what would happen to Christ. The Lord himself mentioned this connection just a few months after John's murder:

> "But I say unto you, That Elias is come already, and they knew him not, but have done unto him whatsoever they listed. <u>Likewise shall also the Son of man suffer of them.</u>" Matthew 17:12

John the Baptist, the one who came in the spirit and power of Elijah, was slain at the hands of evil men.

Feeding the Five Thousand

Thus it would be with the Lord Jesus Christ. "Likewise shall also the Son of man suffer of them." The death of John made Christ acutely aware of the nearness of his own death. This awareness was only accentuated by the coming feast. It was almost the time for passover:

> "And the passover, a feast of the Jews, was nigh."
> John 6:4

Passover was near—the feast which looked ahead to the slaying of the Messiah through the slaying of the lamb. Soon, the blood would be spread upon the posts of the doors (Exodus 12:7) and that blood represented *his blood*. Everything about this feast pointed to the death of the Lord! This was a time of year in which his mind would constantly be reminded of the cross. To add to that, this was the *last* passover which would be celebrated before his crucifixion; Scripture mentions no others until the last supper. There was only one more year before Christ would share the passover meal with his disciples. The Lord could feel the nearness of his death. The forerunner had died, the passover was at hand, and there was only one more year before he would be rejected by his own people and slain at the hands of the Romans.

It was a difficult time for the Lord Jesus. He desired to be alone with his disciples. There was much to say to them, much to be explained about his death and resurrection, and much to encourage about their preaching. Besides private time with the disciples, the Master needed time with his Father. His death was looming on the horizon and he was ever reminded of it—with the death of John and the celebration of the passover feast. This was why Christ crossed over Galilee.

Arrival at the Other Side

And so he and his disciples arrived on the other side of the sea, near the town of Bethsaida.

> "And the apostles when they were returned, told him all that they had done. And he took them, and went aside privately into a desert place belonging to the city called Bethsaida." Luke 9:10

Their little band arrived at a desert place. Now they could have a bit of respite from the crowds, now they could strengthen one another and be reinvigorated. The Lord could meditate upon the Word and spend time in prayer with the Father. Yet sadly, this time was not going to last. As the group landed near Bethsaida, they were met on the shore of the sea by a vast multitude. His time alone with the disciples was not to be.

> "And the people saw them departing, and many knew him, and ran afoot thither out of all cities, and outwent them, and came together unto him. And Jesus, when he came out, saw much people, and was moved with compassion toward them, because they were as sheep not having a shepherd: and he began to teach them many things." Mark 6:33-34

The multitude had actually arrived at the shore before the disciples and their Master! They had originally seen the little group getting into the boat and the crowd had run around the sea quicker than the seasoned fishermen could get the boat to the other side. What an amazing thought! These people were devoted to the idea of seeing the Lord. They longed to be with him—and nothing would stand in their way. This devotion, as was mentioned in an earlier chapter, seems to have originated from the desire to see Christ's miracles:

> "And a great multitude followed him, because they saw his miracles which he did on them that were diseased." John 6:2

The people followed him because they saw his power to heal! In fact, some of the multitude were sick and in need of healing; others were simply friends of the infirm who helped to bring them to the Lord. Matthew explained that when Jesus arrived and saw the multitude before him, he healed their sick:

> "And Jesus went forth, and saw a great multitude, and was moved with compassion toward them, and he healed their sick." Matthew 14:14

It would have been a touching picture. Christ had just crossed the sea of Galilee to be alone with his disciples, but a multitude had followed him and even outran him to the other side—yet it wasn't a multitude of ordinary people, it was filled with people who were desperate and hurting. They were willing to do whatever they needed to do to see the Master—because they wanted to see a miracle and they wanted to be made well. They had rushed ahead simply so that they could see him.

Sheep without a Shepherd

As Christ saw this group of people, he was moved with compassion—and at first it may sound as though this compassion was solely because of all the disease which surrounded him. Perhaps this was true, and the record certainly reads that way in Matthew. However, keep in mind that the Master's focus wasn't always on healing—it was on preaching the Truth. Christ's mind was set on *spiritual* healing. Thus, while Matthew's gospel at first sounds like Christ felt compassion because of the sickness, when Matthew's words are matched up with those of Mark's, the overarching reason for the Lord's compassion becomes more apparent:

> "And Jesus, when he came out, saw much people, and was moved with compassion toward them, because they were <u>as sheep not having a shepherd</u>: and he began to teach them many things." Mark 6:34

As the Lord stepped forth from the boat and looked upon the multitude, he saw them in confusion—as sheep without a shepherd. Truly, they were sincere in what they were seeking—they longed for healing and wholeness; yet the Master something that they needed even more desperately. They needed shepherding. They needed a shepherd to guide them and to teach them the way of peace. They needed a shepherd who would direct them to God, a shepherd who would say "this is the way, walk ye in it." Thus, the record specifically points out that Christ looked upon the multitude with compassion—"because they were as sheep not having a shepherd." This was a deliberate quote of the Old Testament. Mark was seeking to take his readers' minds back to the time of the Exodus, when Moses used this exact same phrase.

> "And Moses spake unto the LORD, saying, Let the LORD, the God of the spirits of all flesh, set a man over the congregation, which may go out before them, and which may lead them out, and which may bring them in; that the congregation of the LORD be

not <u>as sheep which have no shepherd.</u>" Numbers 27:15-17

It was time for Moses to have a successor. He had led the children of Israel out of Egypt and had led them for almost forty years in the wilderness. Now the wilderness wanderings were drawing to a close and a successor needed to be chosen. Pleading with God, Moses asked that the man who was chosen would be a shepherd for Israel—that he would be able to go out and come in before them. He wanted someone that would be a spiritual leader for the nation. If not, the people would be as sheep which had no shepherd. They would be confused and not know what they were to do. As the subsequent verses go on to say, Joshua was the man who was chosen and he succeeded in leading the people uprightly.

Yet this is not the only place where this phrase is used. It appears once more in Scripture—this time used in a slightly different light than the first. Wicked king Ahab of Israel and righteous king Jehoshaphat of Judah had become allies. They were planning an invasion against the kingdom of Syria, and the phrase was used by one of Yahweh's prophets when prophesying about the outcome of the battle.

> "And he said, I saw all Israel scattered upon the hills, <u>as sheep that have not a shepherd</u>: and the LORD said, These have no master: let them return every man to his house in peace." 1 Kings 22:17

This was the prophesy of the battle. It was fulfilled with the death of king Ahab—the children of Israel had no more shepherd. Their leader was dead. Just as Moses had feared when he was pleading with God, the people were confused and lost, there was no one to tell them which way to go. The nation had no king, no ruler. This was the same type of situation which the Lord saw when he looked upon the multitude.

As the boat came to the shore on the other side of Galilee, Jesus saw the multitude—he saw sheep without a shepherd. He saw a group of people who had no leader, and who needed one desperately—not a leader like faithless king Ahab, but a spiritual leader like Joshua. The people needed someone to rekindle their love for the Truth. John the Baptist, one of the great inspirers and great shepherds of the people had just been killed by Herod. Some in that multitude were perhaps even disciples of John. But at that moment, the people had no one to lead them. They had no shepherd.

As they stood before the Lord, he saw their need. He healed them, but more important than their physical healing, he became their shepherd. He guided them toward the Kingdom of God.

> "And the people, when they knew it, followed him: and he received them, and spake unto them <u>of the Kingdom of God</u>, and he healed them that had need of healing." Luke 9:11

When the people were with Christ, he preached. They might have come to find healing or to hear about his power—they would receive those things, but not without the message of the Kingdom. This was what was in the forefront of Christ's mind. He had come to preach the Kingdom of God (Luke 4:43) and the signs which he performed gave credence to his preaching (Acts 2:22). The works reinforced the message, not the other way around. In a day in which some churches seek to make good works and community service the focus of their preaching, we do well to notice this. Jesus kept his focus on the message. People may have been drawn to him because of the miracles (since these were something that no one else could do!), but even when the miracles brought them in, they still found themselves hearing his word.

This was what they needed—this was what would give them life—and the Lord knew it. They were as sheep without a shepherd. They had no direction and they were confused and lost. Christ gave them a direction—the Kingdom of God—and he gave them a powerful taste of that Kingdom as he healed their sicknesses and infirmities.

"Send the Multitude Away…"

As the Lord sat upon the mountain, teaching and healing the people, the day began to wear away—and it seems as though the patience of the disciples began to wear away as well.

> "And when the day began to wear away, then came the twelve, and said unto him, Send the multitude away, that they may go into the towns and country round about, and lodge, and get victuals: for we are here in a desert place." Luke 9:12

"Send the multitude away…" the disciples urged. The words of the disciples immediately sound quite caring and quite noble. They cared about the people and wanted to make sure that they were fed and had a place to sleep. Perhaps these feelings truly were genuine within the hearts of these fishermen. Yet upon further thought, some issues seem to arise in their petition:

- If the people lived in the villages around the sea, surely they would have already known how long it would take them to get home and they would have left at an appropriate time
- If the people became hungry or saw that the time for the closing of the shops was soon, they probably would have left on their own
- If the people were concerned with where they would stay for the night, would they not leave in time to find a place to sleep themselves?

These are just some things to consider when looking at the request of the disciples. It's entirely possible that they were sincere in their petition to the Lord—yet there seem to be some reasons to think differently. Instead, perhaps they were a bit frustrated that they did not get to have their time with Christ as they had initially thought.

As the sun started to drop down in the sky, the disciples begin to get more and more anxious. This was supposed to be their time special with the Lord. This was supposed to be when they could talk to him all about their preaching and the miracles which they performed. This was supposed to be when they could talk to him about John and ask about his death. Yet the multitude was impeding them.

They needed to get the people to leave, so that they could have their time of rest and their time with their Master. "Send them away…" was their plea to Christ.

Feeding the Five Thousand
Buying Bread

This possible frustration of the disciples was a very stark contrast to the attitude of the Lord. Of all of the men in their little band, surely he was the one who could have been the most distressed. His death was only a year away, there was passover to remind him of the cross, and the death of his friend and forerunner was lingering in his mind. He was the one who truly needed a break—yet what did he do when he saw the people? He was filled with compassion, healed them, and spoke to them about the Kingdom.

What an example. May we do the same. Despite hard times, may we continue to work in the service of the Father.

Nevertheless, the disciples, anxiously desiring the multitude to leave, presented their idea to Christ. His response probably came as quite a shock.

> "When Jesus then lifted up his eyes, and saw a great company come unto him, he saith unto Philip, Whence shall we buy bread, that these may eat?" John 6:5

The disciples wanted to send the people away to buy their own bread—and once again, the compassion of the Lord overflowed in his answer. He lifted up his eyes from the disciples to the vast multitude before him and said "Where will we buy bread so that all of these people can eat?" Notice the shift in focus here. The disciples had been thinking about themselves. They had wanted the multitude to leave so that they could spend private time with the Master. Yet this was not the way that an *apostle* of Christ should think. All throughout this lesson, the Lord Jesus began to teach his disciples to think like *apostles*. Christ shifted the focus of the request off of the disciples and their desire to send away the multitude, and he focused it on the people who needed a shepherd. Instead of wanting the people to go away and buy bread, the disciples needed to think about providing the bread *for* them. Matthew's account includes a statement of Christ which helps to make the focus of his reply even more clear:

> "But Jesus said unto them, They need not depart; give ye them to eat." Matthew 14:16

The disciples had been thinking about themselves and their own wants. They simply wanted the multitude to go away. Yet in order to get their thinking to align more with the thinking of an apostle, Christ specifically addressed their wrong ideas—"They need not depart." Instead, they were to shift the focus off of their desires and think about how they could help lead and inspire these people toward the Kingdom of God. "Give ye them to eat." They needed to feed the multitude. How was this possible? The question was a test for their faith, because Christ already had a plan:

> "And this he said to prove him: for he himself knew what he would do." John 6:6

In the gospel of John, the Lord specifically directed his question towards Philip, yet based off of Andrew's response, the question was heard by more than just him. The disciples would have been incredulous! How could the Lord Jesus expect them to feed all of these people?! There were thousands of them! Yet it was a test to get

Feeding the Five Thousand

them to think by faith and to remember the power of the one who was standing by them.

> "Philip answered him, Two hundred pennyworth of bread is not sufficient for them, that every one of them may take a little." John 6:7

When asked the question, Philip tried to think over the figures. He staggered in unbelief at how much all of it would cost. Two hundred pennyworth! In the gospel of Matthew, in the parable of the vineyard, Christ spoke about a penny being approximately a day's wage (Matthew 20:2). If this is accurate, this amount was almost a year's wage! There was no way that this could be done. The disciples could not afford that. Yet at the same time, Andrew heard the discussion that the Lord was having with Philip, and he walked up with a young boy next to him:

> "One of his disciples, Andrew, Simon Peter's brother, saith unto him, there is a lad here, which hath five barley loaves, and two small fishes: but what are they among so many?" John 6:8-9

Andrew walked up with a lad who had two barley loaves and two fishes. These were offered to Christ, yet again with an attitude of disbelief—"but what are they among so many?" Andrew's suggestion and the sudden appearance of the lad are quite intriguing. They bring certain questions to mind:

- Where did the lad come from? Was he someone who was about to eat his dinner, and Andrew suddenly snatched him away?

- Why did a young man have five loaves of bread and two fish to eat? That's a huge amount of food for one person!

In seeking to answer these questions, a thought is advanced for consideration. Perhaps this lad was actually a young servant whom the disciples had told to go to Bethsaida and buy them bread. When thinking of the story in this light, different parts of the story start to come together and some of the questions begin to be answered. Suddenly, the remark of Christ, "Give ye them to eat," becomes more believable. He was looking at a group of disciples whom he knew had gone out and bought bread. They actually *had bread* that they could give to the people! In the gospel of Mark, the five loaves and the two fish actually appear as a response to one of Christ's questions:

> "He answered and said unto them, Give ye them to eat. And they say unto him, Shall we go and buy two hundred pennyworth of bread, and give them to eat? He saith unto them, How many loaves have ye? go and see. And when they knew, they say, Five, and two fishes." Mark 6:37-38

Christ specifically asked them, "how many loaves do you have, go and see." This could not possibly have been referring to how much food the people in the multitude had. Clearly, the disciples did not go from person to person asking them how much food they had—if they did do something like that, they would not have come back with only *one* person and only five loaves and two fish. Surely a multitude of more than five thousand people would have had more than that among themselves.

Feeding the Five Thousand

The Lord's question was specifically directed to the disciples, probably because he knew that the disciples had just sent out someone to go buy food on their behalf. They didn't yet know how much their money had bought, thus their having to check how much they had. This understanding is confirmed by the record in both Matthew and Luke as well:

> "But Jesus said unto them, They need not depart; give ye them to eat. And they say unto him, We have here but five loaves, and two fishes." Matthew 14:16-17

> "But he said unto them, Give ye them to eat. And they said, We have no more but five loaves and two fishes; except we should go and buy meat for all this people." Luke 9:13

The disciples were the ones who had the five loaves and two fish. The lad had arrived with the basket and was then brought to the Lord—in response to the question "How many loaves have ye?" Again, this was why the lad had so much food—it wasn't for himself. It was for the twelve to share. This was also probably why Andrew brought the lad to Christ with such an attitude of disbelief, saying, "but what are they among so many?" He wasn't urging that the five loaves and two fish be used to feed the multitude—he was bringing the lad because that is what Christ asked, "How many loaves have ye?"

What a lesson in sacrifice this would have been for the disciples. They had originally pleaded that the multitude be sent away so that they might have some special time with the Lord. They had bought bread and fish for themselves so that they might have food—yet the

Master was chipping away at all of their thoughts about their own wants and their own needs. "Give ye them to eat…" Not only would the multitude not be sent home, but the disciples themselves would have to provide the bread and fish for the miracle. The Lord was shifting their thoughts off of themselves and toward those whom they needed to serve. They were being taught how to be apostles rather than disciples.

The Feeding

The disciples had just given up their meal for the sake of the people—getting a taste of what Christ had said a year prior, "my meat is to do the will of him that sent me." They would have wondered what it was that their Master was planning. How would he feed this massive swarm of people with just five loaves and two fish? The miracle was about to begin:

> "And Jesus said, Make the men sit down. Now there was much grass in the place. So the men sat down, in number about five thousand. And Jesus took the loaves; and when he had given thanks, he distributed to the disciples, and the disciples to them that were set down; and likewise of the fishes as much as they would." John 6:10-11

The disciples were given the task of making the multitude sit down. Then, after everyone was seated, the Lord Jesus gave thanks to his Father for the food, the loaves and fish were distributed to the disciples, and then the disciples brought them to all of the people. Again, they were being trained for the time when Christ would no longer be with them. It was their job to distribute the food because only a year later, they would be given the task of distributing spiritual food throughout all the world. They would be the ones who would be shepherds to the sheep who had just lost their shepherd:

> "So when they had dined, Jesus saith to Simon Peter, Simon, son of Jonas, lovest thou me more than these? He saith unto him, Yea, Lord; thou knowest that I love thee. He saith unto him, <u>Feed my lambs</u>." John 21:15

The disciples would have the task of feeding the sheep. Now at the feeding of the multitude, they were given practice—they distributed the food all throughout the ranks of people. Everyone received as much bread and as much fish as they desired. What a bewildered group of disciples would have come back to the Lord at the end of the miracle! Truly, their fives loaves and two fish had fed the multitude, just as Christ had said—"Give ye them to eat." They would have stood in awe at the man who had the power to create a meal for over five thousand people out of a meal for just twelve. Yet the Lord was not finished teaching them.

> "When they were filled, he said unto his disciples, Gather up the fragments that remain, that nothing be lost. Therefore they gathered them together, and filled twelve baskets with the fragments of the five barley loaves, which remained over and above unto them that had eaten." John 6:12-13

After the people had eaten, it was time to collect the fragments which remained. None of them were to be lost. Thus, each disciple went forth with their basket and began to collect. Astonishingly, all of them came back with full baskets. Imagine the reaction of the disciples as they mulled over what had just taken place—they had given up their fives loaves and two fishes and now they were holding *twelve baskets* full of loaves and fish. This wasn't just Christ being frugal—this was another lesson for the disciples! In their sacrifice, they had received much more than they had initially given.

How they would have marveled! This was just a small lesson for them in the work of apostleship. The life of an apostle would not be easy and many things would have to be given up for the sake of the flock. Yet the end result is so much greater than what was ever given. Despite the sacrifices which are made throughout life, the service of an apostle culminates in the glory of the Kingdom of God.

The people ate the food and had enough. Even the disciples had eaten the food and had enough. Now they had collected up the fragments of the bread and realized that they finished with more than which they had started. It was a great day of learning for the disciples, and yet at the same time, it should have been a great day of learning for the multitude as well. As mentioned earlier, the Lord always used his signs to emphasize the message. This miracle was not an exception. Here, he sought to lift the minds of the multitude above—to get them to see what he had come to accomplish—not the work of a king, not the work of a ruler, but the work of a lamb.

The Lamb of God

Truly, it was a passover feast right before their eyes. Passover was nigh and the multitudes were sharing bread together. Even the time of day fit perfectly.

> "And ye shall keep it up until the fourteenth day of the same month: and the whole assembly of the congregation of Israel shall kill it <u>between the two evenings</u>." Exodus 12:6 margin

The passover lamb was to be slain "between the two evenings." This was exactly the time of day in which the feeding of the five thousand took place. Notice that Matthew actually mentioned both of these evenings in his record:

> "<u>And when it was evening</u>, his disciples came to him, saying, This is a desert place, and the time is now past; send the multitude away, that they may go into the villages, and buy themselves victuals." Matthew 14:15

When the disciples came to Christ and asked him to send away the multitude, Matthew specifically wrote that it was evening time. The chapter then goes on to record the feeding of the five thousand, and shortly after the miracle finished, the second evening appears:

> "And when he had sent the multitudes away, he went up into a mountain apart to pray: and when the evening was come, he was there alone." Matthew 14:23

After the multitudes departed, Jesus went up into a mountain. It is at this point that Matthew said that the evening came! This was not a mistake, but rather a direct allusion back to passover! The feeding of the five thousand happened *directly* between the "two evenings." This was a passover meal. Through the miracle, the Lord sought to draw the peoples' thoughts back to passover. The feast was near, it was the right time of day, and they had the bread before them—all that was missing was the lamb. That was the point.

The Lord Jesus Christ was the lamb.

John the Baptist also sought to make this connection (John 1:29, 36) when he proclaimed, "Behold the Lamb of God, which taketh away the sin of the world." This miracle was to show the people that Jesus had come as a lamb. He had come to be offered and slain, just as the passover lamb. This miracle was supposed to cause the people to think, "it's passover time, we have the bread before us, the timing is perfect for passover, yet where is the lamb?" Unfortunately, many of them didn't make the connection. Instead of recognizing Christ's role as the lamb who would be slain, they saw him as their deliverer and the one who would throw off the Roman oppression. He could heal all of their wounds from battle and he could supply them with endless provisions. Surely he could overcome the Roman hordes.

Making a King

> "Then those men, when they had seen the miracle that Jesus did, said, This is of a truth that prophet that should come into the world. When Jesus therefore perceived that they would come and take him by force, to make him a king, he departed again into a mountain himself alone." John 6:14-15

He would be their king. Never had they seen a man who could do such signs—this was what they had been waiting for! They knew that their Messiah was near (Luke 3:15) and they were waiting for him to come and take the throne as King of the Jews. Now, here they were, seated near the sea of Galilee, eating "endless" food, having their infirmities healed, hearing about the Kingdom of God, and as Luke wrote, sitting in ranks of fifties:

> "For they were about five thousand men. And he said to his disciples, Make them sit down by fifties in a company. And they did so, and made them all sit down." Luke 9:14-15

The people were sitting in companies of fifty—and that seating arrangement could have done quite a bit to excite the crowds. Throughout Israel's history, the basic squadron was about that size! The armies during the Old Testament were typically comprised of bands of fifties. Here are some examples:

- Ahaziah continuously sent groups of fifty men to come and take Elijah:

> "Then the king sent unto him a captain of fifty <u>with his fifty</u>. And he went up to him: and, behold, he sat on the top of an hill. And he spake unto him, Thou man of God, the king hath said, Come down." 2 Kings 1:9

The first squadron which Ahaziah sent to Elijah was made up of fifty men and one commander. It was the same with the second:

> "Again also he sent unto him another captain of fifty <u>with his fifty</u>. And he answered and said unto him, O man of God, thus hath the king said, Come down quickly." 2 Kings 1:11

The second squadron was the same as the first—and so was the third.

"And he sent again a captain of the third fifty <u>with his fifty</u>. And the third captain of fifty went up, and came and fell on his knees before Elijah, and besought him, and said unto him, O man of God, I pray thee, let my life, and the life of these fifty thy servants, be precious in thy sight." 2 Kings 1:13

- God spoke about destroying Jerusalem and Judah, and one of the things He said He would destroy was their "captain of fifty":

"For, behold, the Lord, the LORD of hosts, doth take away from Jerusalem and from Judah the stay and the staff, the whole stay of bread, and the whole stay of water...<u>the captain of fifty</u>, and the honorable man, and the counsellor, and the cunning artificer, and the eloquent orator." Isaiah 3:1, 3

As the people sat upon the grass, divided up into these groups of fifties, they may have looked around and seen an army! At the front of them was a man who would lead them against the Romans and one who could use his miraculous power to make them well nigh invincible. This man must be their Messiah sent from God! This was the one who would set up the Kingdom right before them. This was the one who would be their king! Thus, why would they waste time? They wanted to crown him immediately.

This was an unacceptable reaction on the part of the people. The Lord had not come to make them an invincible army to fight against the Romans. He hadn't even organized them in groups for the purpose of

Feeding the Five Thousand

making them look like an army. Rather, he organized them into "ranks" (Mark 6:40), or "garden plots" as the word means, to get them to see their connection to the "green grass" (Mark 6:39) upon which they were sitting. "All flesh is grass," said the prophet, "the grass withereth, the flower fadeth" (Isaiah 40:6-8). Christ sought to focus the minds of the people upon their need for salvation. There they were, sitting upon the green grass in "garden plots"—demonstrating that they themselves would wither and perish, just as the grass. They needed Christ for salvation—not as the captain for their army against the Romans.

He would not be their king at this time. He had a greater work to accomplish at Jerusalem and how he was straightened till it was accomplished. With reminders of his death looming all around him, the Lord did not need a "way out" from the people. He did not need the added temptation of becoming their king immediately. It was time for prayer to the Father. It was time to be alone with the God of all comforts.

> "And straightway Jesus constrained his disciples to get into a ship, and to go before him unto the other side, while he sent the multitudes away. And when he had sent the multitudes away, he went up into a mountain apart to pray: and when the evening was come, he was there alone." Matthew 14:22-23

The multitude was sent away and the disciples were *constrained* to get into the boat. Not even his closest twelve understood his mission at his first coming. They too saw him as the king (John 1:49), they looked for him to soon bring the kingdom (Acts 1:6), and they could not wait until they could get their position therein (Matthew 18:1, Matthew 20:20-23). For this reason,

Jesus also sent the disciples away. They would not get their special time with the Master. They were constrained to get into the boat and row towards the Capernaum.

Jesus now had time alone with his Father.

The Parable

That's the story of the feeding of the five thousand. There is much to think about and much to put together. Yet again, it was a sign—it was a parable. There is a hidden story beneath all that took place at Bethsaida that day.

As mentioned earlier, this examination of the parable will be slightly different than the exposition of the story. For the parable, the focus will be exclusively on the details from the gospel of John. John was the one who recorded the parable—thus, he dropped certain details and added others in accordance with the deeper meaning that he sought to show.

The Bread

One of the simplest things to interpret when looking at this parable is the bread. The Lord gave the interpretation of it just a few verses later in the chapter:

> "<u>I am the living bread</u> which came down from heaven: if any man eat of this bread, he shall live for ever: and <u>the bread that I will give is my flesh</u>, which I will give for the life of the world." John 6:51

Feeding the Five Thousand

The bread is the flesh of the Master—the flesh which was broken to give life. This entire miracle and parable revolve around an understanding of this symbol. The feeding of the five thousand was about the sacrifice of Christ.

As the Lord broke the bread and distributed it to the people, it was a picture of his flesh being broken on the cross and the bread of life being distributed throughout all the world. This was why John specifically sought to give the reader an understanding of the priceless worth of the bread:

> "Philip answered him, Two hundred pennyworth of bread is not sufficient for them, that every one of them may take a little." John 6:7

The figure which was thrown out by Philip was an impossible figure for the disciples to muster—it was too much! Buying bread for the multitude would have been so expensive that the idea was entirely unfathomable to Philip. The bread which was distributed on that mountainside had a huge value! So it was with the bread of life—the Lord Jesus Christ. His devoted life was a priceless treasure.

> "Forasmuch as ye knew that ye were not redeemed with corruptible things, as silver and gold, from your vain conversation received by tradition from your father; but with the precious blood of Christ, as of a lamb without blemish and without spot." 1 Peter 1:18-19

We were not redeemed with mere corruptible things, but instead with the precious blood of Christ—a treasure more precious than any of the things which perish. Just like the priceless bread, Christ's sacrifice was not something which we could "afford."

Yet again, just like his sacrifice, the bread was something which was limitless—no matter how many people arrived, there was bread for everyone. Even if there had been fifty thousand people, or five hundred thousand people, there would have been enough for everyone to be filled. That's the beauty of the sacrifice of Christ. There isn't just a set number of people who can enjoy it. It's for everyone who desires to take part and who seeks after the Lord.

In addition to the value of the bread and its limitlessness, John made another intriguing connection to Christ. Out of all of the gospel writers, only John mentioned that the loaves were made out of barley.

Barley Bread

> "There is a lad here, which hath five <u>barley</u> loaves, and two small fishes: but what are they among so many?" John 6:9

The loaves which the disciples had purchased were specifically barley loaves. Barley bread wasn't fancy nor was it expensive. In fact, during the days of Elisha, barley sold for half of the price of flour:

> "And it came to pass as the man of God had spoken to the king, saying, Two measures of barley for a shekel, and a measure of fine flour for a shekel, shall be to morrow about this time in the gate of Samaria." 2 Kings 7:18

Feeding the Five Thousand

Between barley and flour, barley was the cheaper type of grain. It was a humble food which could be accessed by all of the people—just like the Lord Jesus. Again, the same idea is shown in the book of Revelation:

> "And I heard a voice in the midst of the four beasts say, A measure of wheat for a penny, and three measures of barley for a penny; and see thou hurt not the oil and the wine." Revelation 6:6

One measure of wheat could be bought for a penny, yet three measures of barley could be purchased for the same price. Barley bread was therefore the cheaper bread which people could buy. It wasn't fancy bread, but it was the humble bread. The same can be said about the Lord Jesus. Though he was rich, he became poor for our sake. He took upon himself the form of a servant. Our Lord Jesus was the barley bread, which was broken upon the mountain and distributed to a multitude.

Two Fish

Yet the bread was not distributed alone. Along with it came the fish. While the Lord was represented in the bread, the fish represented something very different. Looking throughout Scripture, fish are constantly representative of people. In Matthew 13:47-50, Christ told the parable of the net, in which people were captured as fish and either kept or thrown out at judgment. The words of Habakkuk reinforce this idea:

> "And makest men as the fishes of the sea, as the creeping things, that have no ruler over them?" Habakkuk 1:14

Habakkuk compared men and fish. In Scripture, fish are symbolic of men, or of people. Hence, the term used by Christ, "fishers of men." The two fish which are seen, then, in the story of the feeding of the five thousand are the two groups of people who are connected to the sacrifice of Christ. It is the Jews and the Gentiles. Both of these groups are intimately connected to the distributing of the bread—Christ died for both the Jew and the Gentile.

This is not to say that the Jews and the Gentiles were part of Christ's sacrifice and that they were distributed along with the bread. The point is that the two fish are connected to the bread—the Jews and Gentiles are connected to the sacrifice of Christ.

The Fragments

Once the fish and the bread were distributed to the multitude, Christ sent his disciples out to collect the fragments.

> "When they were filled, he said unto his disciples, Gather up the fragments that remain, <u>that nothing be lost</u>. Therefore they gathered them together, and filled twelve baskets with the fragments of the five barley loaves, which remained over and above unto them that had eaten." John 6:12-13

The Lord Jesus wanted nothing to be lost. Thus, the disciples went through all of the ranks of people and gathered the fragments back. It's quite a curious thing to do—yet there was a meaning beneath all of it. Notice that in his later discourse, Christ seemed to almost quote himself about the gathering of the fragments:

> "And this is the Father's will which hath sent me, that of all which he hath given me I should lose nothing, but should raise it up again at the last day." John 6:39

Again, he brought up this idea of losing nothing, yet instead of applying it to bread, he applied it to his followers (which are aptly described as his body elsewhere in Scripture; 1 Corinthians 12:27). Later in John's gospel, the Lord used the same phraseology again with a similar interpretation:

> "While I was with them in the world, I kept them in thy name: those that thou gavest me I have kept, and none of them is lost, but the son of perdition; that the scripture might be fulfilled." John 17:12

Here, the concept of losing nothing is again applied to Christ's followers—but this time it is even slightly more specific as to which followers it refers. Out of his disciples, those who were part of his ecclesia, part of his body, he would lose nothing—except the son of perdition. The fragments represent the disciples! After his death, when the disciples were desperately struggling to understand why their Messiah had died, the Lord gathered them together, appearing in his immortal and resurrected state—giving them strength so that none of them would be lost.

> "Then the same day at evening, being the first day of the week, when the doors were shut where the disciples were assembled for fear of the Jews, came Jesus and stood in the midst, and saith unto them, Peace be unto you." John 20:19

Despite their confusion over the death of their Redeemer, the disciples still gathered together. It was at this gathering that the Lord Jesus appeared and encouraged his disciples so that none of them would be lost. He lifted them up from their despair and gave them hope once again. He showed them that he had been raised to immortality and incorruption!

> "And that he was buried, and that he rose again the third day according to the scriptures: and that he was seen of Cephas, <u>then of the twelve</u>." 1 Corinthians 15:4-5

The disciples were gathered together and saw Christ after his resurrection! Through this they were given strength so that none of them would be lost. This last verse also gives an additional connection to the gathering up of the fragments. Notice that when referring to the disciples it calls them "the twelve." Yet when Christ appeared to the disciples after his resurrection, it doesn't seem as though he actually appeared to all twelve! Judas hung himself fairly promptly after the death of Christ (Matthew 27:3-5)—but 1 Corinthians 15 mentions "the twelve." The probable reason for this is that "the twelve" is Scripture's way of referencing the disciples, even if there were only eleven at that point (cp. John 20:24). This connects right back to the parable of the five thousand. When the fragments were collected, notice how many baskets were filled—twelve, fitting perfectly with the disciples.

Thus, the fragments represent the disciples and their gathering together after the death of Christ. They would be brought back together and strengthened so that none, save the son of perdition, would be lost.

Feeding the Five Thousand

The Jews

Finally, one of the most important things to note about the parable is its context. Again, just like the parable of the man at Bethesda, this allegory is surrounded by criticisms of the corrupted Jewish law and its followers. The parable begins by mentioning that a *feast of the Jews* was at hand—just like the story one chapter prior:

> "And the passover, a feast of the Jews, was nigh." John 6:4

This feast should have been Yahweh's feast, yet it wasn't. It had become a feast of the Jews. As well, the picture is closed by Christ's condemnation of the Jews and their focus on material blessings and works:

> "Jesus answered them and said, Verily, verily, I say unto you, Ye seek me, not because ye saw the miracles, but because ye did eat of the loaves, and were filled." John 6:26

The people were coming for the wrong reason! They followed him because of his miraculous abilities! They were not seeking to come nearer to God—they simply wanted more food. Their coming to Christ was not motivated by belief:

> "But I said unto you, That ye also have seen me, and believe not." John 6:36

Jesus condemned the lack of belief in these people. Because the parable of the feeding of the five thousand is surrounded by negativity toward the faithless Jews of those days, it is clear that the parable will also have the same inclination.

> "When Jesus therefore perceived that they would come and take him by force, to make him a king, he departed again into a mountain himself alone." John 6:15

Not understanding what was taking place before them, the Jews sought to enforce their perception of God's plan. They were going to make Christ their king. This was the exact same thing that happened after the sacrifice of Christ—perfectly fitting the timing of the parable. All throughout the Acts of the Apostles, the Jews continuously used force in order to uphold their understanding of God's ways. They persecuted the disciples, even to the point of stoning the apostle Paul (Acts 14:19).

Summary of Parable

In the feeding of the five thousand, we have a parable much the same as the others. The parable tells a story—the story of the death of Christ, the gathering of his disciples after his resurrection, and the force used by the Jews during the first century. The focus of this miracle is Christ's sacrifice. It shows the Lord's death and the events which followed. It is this death which is one of the main messages of the gospel—the things concerning the kingdom of God and the name of Jesus Christ (Acts 8:12). This is why this miracle is mentioned in all four gospels! It is the axis upon which the entire gospel revolves! Without the work of Jesus Christ and without his second coming, there would be no gospel.

Feeding the Five Thousand

This parable is a quick snapshot of the sacrifice of the Lord Jesus and the events which shortly followed. Yet the parable isn't over. The next event in the gospel of John, the walking on the water, takes this picture and adds upon it. It starts with the sacrifice of Christ as the background and beautifully builds upon that story.

Chapter 5
Walking on Water

The multitude teemed with excitement as they thought about what they had just witnessed. A mighty miracle had taken place before their eyes—they had seen the Lord's powers in creating food, seen his abilities for healing, and perceived that he had set them down together as an army. They were ready to make the Master their king, storm through the land of Israel and push out the oppressive Romans. This was what the people had been waiting for! For years they had looked for their Messiah—the one who would be their deliverer. Finally, in the Lord Jesus, they believed that they had found their man. He would fulfill the prophecies of Israel's restoration. He would reign on David's throne. He would conquer every enemy.

This was a tune which would ring close to the hearts of the disciples. Just like the masses of Israel, the disciples themselves also looked for the immediate return of the Kingdom of God (Luke 19:11, Acts 1:6). They saw Christ as their king—and in order to be a king, one must have a kingdom! In their minds, the time in which Christ would throw off his poverty and take over as king was only a matter of days or months. The twelve would have looked upon the clamoring multitude and their desire to take Christ and make him king—and they would have supported the movement. The disciples had been waiting for a day such as this.

How it would have excited them as they gathered the fragments and heard whispers travel throughout the multitude. "This is of a truth that prophet that should come into the world..." How they would have been filled with nervous energy as the whispers of the Lord's Messiahship started to get louder and the multitude began to turn towards the Master—this could be it! The Kingdom of God may have only been hours or minutes away!

Yet these hopes would have been shattered as the Lord quickly perceived what was spreading throughout the multitude.

> "When Jesus therefore perceived that they would come and take him by force, to make him a king, he departed again into a mountain himself alone." John 6:15

The Lord would not allow this type of movement to take place. Truly, he was the heir to David's throne. Truly, he was the one "whose right it is." Yet now was not the time. The same temptation had come to him two years earlier and he had denied it—but by no means was he then immune to that temptation! Despite how he may have wanted to save his people from their oppressors, this was not in accordance with the plan of God and he needed to fight against the urge to accept the crown from the people. He needed time alone with his Father.

> "And straightway Jesus constrained his disciples to get into a ship, and to go before him unto the other side, while he sent the multitudes away." Matthew 14:22

The Lord did not waste any time. As soon as he perceived what was taking place, he *immediately* constrained the twelve to enter into the boat. One can only imagine the protests which would have issued from the disciples' lips. Yet Christ "constrained" them. He literally had to force them to depart—he did not need his closest friends urging him against God's plan. Instead, they were to go to Capernaum, a city a little ways to the west, and they would "go before him." He would send the multitude away, spend some time alone, and then meet them on the "other side."

The plan was set, yet it seems as though the disciples were not altogether convinced that it was a good idea. Later in the chapter, Mark wrote of the general attitude of the disciples at this point:

> "For they considered not the miracle of the loaves: <u>for their heart was hardened</u>." Mark 6:52

Something about the hearts of the disciples hindered their spiritual perception—more than likely it was their desire for the Lord Jesus to become king over Israel and to bring the Kingdom of God. No doubt they were frustrated that he had not accepted the desire of the multitude and had chosen to send everyone away. Perhaps this was why the Master himself, upon seeing many of his followers leave him, turned to his disciples and asked them if they too would depart:

> "From that time many of his disciples went back, and walked no more with him. Then said Jesus unto the twelve, Will ye also go away?" John 6:66-67

Many of his disciples were turning their backs upon him—and the Lord Jesus Christ looked upon the twelve and asked them if they too would choose to leave. There must have been some hint of frustration or disillusionment within the heart of the twelve to cause the Lord to ask this. After the feeding of the five thousand, a confused and frustrated group of men sailed across the sea of Galilee—they knew that Jesus was their Messiah and they trusted him (Matthew 14:28), yet they didn't understand his resistance to take the throne.

Throughout the next year, they would likely look back to this day as the one in which Christ allowed the kingship to pass through his fingers. It would be a day of sadness for them, and a day of frustration.

Nevertheless they reluctantly began the voyage from Bethsaida to Capernaum.

On a Mountain

Meanwhile, Jesus turned his attention to the crowds. It was imperative that they were dispersed—before they were able to put their plan into action. He would send them away and then go off alone by himself.

> "And when he had sent the multitudes away, he went up into a mountain apart to pray: and when the evening was come, he was there alone." Matthew 14:23

The day was drawing to a close and the Lord was on a mountain by himself. Here, he could have solace and commune with his Father. He could pour out his heart. The day had been immensely trying—first with the news of John's death and the passover reminding him of the nearness of the cross, and second with the multitude seeking to proclaim him as their king. As an inspiring example, the Master turned to the only source of true comfort and spent the night in prayer.

Struggle at Sea

While the Lord found comfort through his Father, the disciples found something altogether different. In the beginning, the voyage had likely been fairly routine. A number of the disciples were experienced fishermen, so sailing late at night would not have been something new. As well, a least a handful of their little group was actually from the area and familiar with the sea of Galilee:

> "And Jesus, walking by the sea of Galilee, saw two brethren, Simon called Peter, and Andrew his brother, casting a net into the sea: for they were fishers. And he saith unto them, Follow me, and I will make you fishers of men. And they straightway left their nets, and followed him. And going on from thence, he saw other two brethren, James the son of Zebedee, and John his brother, in a ship with Zebedee their father, mending their nets; and he called them." Matthew 4:18-21

Both Peter and Andrew, and James and John had all been fishermen *upon the sea of Galilee*. To add to that, Philip was from Bethsaida (John 12:21)—the town nearest the feeding of the five thousand. Almost half of the disciples would have been familiar with this body of water and would have had no qualms about sailing upon it. Yet unbeknownst to them, their day was going to become even more difficult. A storm had quickly developed upon the sea—the wind began blowing hard against them and the waves tossed their boat to and fro:

Walking on Water

> "But the ship was now in the midst of the sea, tossed with waves: for the wind was contrary."
> Matthew 14:24

The disciples had been able to make it to the middle of the sea—yet they could seem to go no further. Despite their skills on the sea and despite their knowledge of sailing, they were stuck in the center of this body of water. They were in "the midst of the sea"—the absolute furthest from land that they had been since their trip began. With the wind pushing against them, their sails were useless, and all they could do was try to row themselves to the shore. How agonizing this would have been for them! They were already weary from the day, they were confused about the death of John, they were not able to have their alone time with Jesus, their Master had refused the crown, and now they were rowing for their lives upon the sea. This day had been filled with one trial after the other. Christ was on the other side, and they were alone. Oh that the Lord was with them! Though he had frustrated them, they still longed to be with him. He had once calmed the storm before their eyes (Matthew 8:26); he could have saved them from this tempest. Yet he was as far from them as the other side of the sea. Their only hope was to pray to the Father and row with all of their might.

The experience of the disciples was drastically different from the experience of the Lord Jesus. While he was being strengthened, they were being battered—yet though they may have felt alone, their Messiah knew their troubles. They were not altogether without help. From high up on the mountain, praying to the God of Israel, the Lord Jesus Christ could see his twelve disciples toiling upon the sea. He could see their troubles and could envision their agony.

> "<u>And he saw them toiling in rowing</u>; for the wind was contrary unto them: and about the fourth watch of the night he cometh unto them, walking upon the sea, and would have passed by them." Mark 6:48

As their little boat went up on the side of a swell and crashed down upon the other, the disciples were not alone. The Lord saw their troubles—much as he sees ours today. Yet the disciples had no idea. As far as they could tell, he was nowhere to be seen.

> "And entered into a ship, and went over the sea toward Capernaum. And it was now dark, <u>and Jesus was not come to them.</u>" John 6:17

There they were, waiting for him to come and join them, yet there was no sign of him. They longed for him to be with them, but they had no idea where he was. As the hours went by and the storm continued, the disciples kept looking for the Master, yet he was no where to be seen. As far as they could tell, there was *nothing else* out on the water. Many of the other boats had headed back to shore (John 6:23). They were there alone, being cast about by the waves, striving to row back to shore.

Walking on Water

While the disciples had been rowing in the midst of the sea for the better part of the night, the Lord was still in prayer. Having poured out his heart to the Father, he finished his prayer and turned his attention to the twelve:

> "And he saw them toiling in rowing; for the wind was contrary unto them: and about the fourth watch of the night he cometh unto them, walking upon the sea, and would have passed by them." Mark 6:48

It was the fourth watch of the night—approximately 3:00-6:00 in the morning. The disciples had been rowing all throughout the night and the situation was probably becoming fairly desperate. The twelve had no idea how they would weather out the storm. But the Lord Jesus Christ knew their trials and would deliver them. As he went out to them on the sea, he didn't use a boat. Unlike anyone had ever seen before, he began to step upon the water—and he didn't sink. Step after step he continued to walk upon the sea. The wind howled and the waves crashed around him—but none of them disturbed the Son of God. Here is a picture of the perfect peace which is derived from prayer with the God of all comfort.

Peacefully walking upon the troubled sea, the Lord Jesus began to make his way towards his agonized disciples. Yet strangely enough, as Mark wrote, the Master "would have passed by them." As he was going to rescue his followers, he made it appear as though he was just going to pass by them to the other side—possibly because he wanted them to call him back and acknowledge their need for him. When they had parted from him earlier in the evening, the parting had not been pleasant—the disciples were frustrated and annoyed at the command of the Lord. Perhaps he didn't want to look as though he was going straight towards them and planning to rescue them—he wanted them to see him, find out that it was him, and seek to be with him.

The presence of the Lord would have been the first thing that the disciples desired. If only they could meet up with their Messiah. All around them, they could only see the roaring waves and the blackness of the sky. There were no boats and nothing to give them hope of being near the shore. Yet as they continued toiling, they saw something off to the side. They couldn't quite make out the form of it, but it looked like a man!

> "But when they saw him walking upon the sea, they supposed it had been a spirit, and cried out." Mark 6:49

The disciples were completely caught off guard by what they saw! Weary and worn out from their intense day, and their long night rowing, they weren't quite sure what it was that they saw! Just imagine the cry coming forth from their vessel as the first disciple spotted the shadowy figure and alerted the rest of the men. They could tell that it was the form of a man—but how could it be hovering upon the water in this way? Why were the waves not slamming it down into the deep? How could it withstand the wind?

The form was passing by them when they first saw it, but as soon as they cried out—it turned towards them and spoke.

> "For they all saw him, and were troubled. And immediately he walked with them, and saith unto them, Be of good cheer: it is I; be not afraid." Mark 6:50

Walking on Water

The actual words of the Master here are quite intriguing and give a powerful meaning to what it was that he was possibly trying to convey to his disciples. Green's Literal Translation gives a literal rendition of what Christ said:

> "For all saw Him, and were troubled. And immediately He spoke to them and said to them, Have courage. <u>I AM</u>! Do not fear." Mark 6:50 LITV

At first, this rendering may seem as though it actually makes the meaning *more* confusing, rather than more plain. However, when this passage is compared to other scriptures in which the Lord said something similar, a striking meaning arises. Throughout the gospels, the Lord made a number of statements in which he proclaimed "I am"—but many of these passages make much more sense if he meant "I am the Christ," or "I am he"—many Christians would rather make him out to say "I am God," but that typically doesn't make sense in the context. Because of this, in a number of those passages, the translators of the AV have correctly added the "he" to Christ's "I am" statements. Here are two examples:

> "Then said Jesus unto them, When ye have lifted up the Son of man, then shall ye know that <u>I am he</u>, and that I do nothing of myself; but as my Father hath taught me, I speak these things." John 8:28

"Then shall ye know that I am he." The "he" there is not in the original and is italicized in the KJV. It should read "Then shall ye know that I am." Was the Lord trying to assert that he was God? Well, when Christ was lifted up, no one of record was convinced that he was God, or the Father. Rather, they came to believe that he was the Son of God (cp. Matthew 27:54)—they recognized him as the Christ! When the Lord here said "I am," he didn't mean that he was God, he meant that he was the Christ. The same can be seen in this next example:

> "I speak not of you all: I know whom I have chosen: but that the scripture may be fulfilled, He that eateth bread with me hath lifted up his heel against me. Now I tell you before it come, that, when it is come to pass, ye may believe <u>that I am he</u>." John 13:18-19

Again, the "he" is not in the original. Was the Lord stating that he was the Christ, or that he was God? Once this passage is examined, the answer must be the former! Here, the Lord Jesus Christ quoted a passage from Psalm 41 which was specifically *a reference to the Messiah*—not to God! Thus, when the passage was fulfilled, the disciples could see the fulfillment and believe that he was the Christ! When the Master used the phrase "I am" in the gospels, he wasn't seeking to show that he was God or part of the Trinity, but instead he was seeking to show that he was the Messiah—the Anointed One! He was the Christ! This is how the Lord's statement to the disciples when he was walking on the water should be understood. He was telling them that he was the Christ! Young's Literal Translation validates this understanding, because it adds the "he" after "I am":

> "For they all saw him, and were troubled, and immediately he spake with them, and saith to them, 'Take courage, I am he, be not afraid.'" Mark 6:50 YLT

Throughout the night the disciples had been frustrated and couldn't understand why the Lord Jesus had refused the throne of Israel—perhaps he wasn't actually the Messiah? Perhaps they had been mistaken. These words of the Lord would have helped to calm their fears. He was the Christ. He was the redeemer of Israel. He was the Son of God—their hopes and lives had not been placed upon the wrong man. This was exactly how the disciples interpreted his words (Matthew 14:33).

Peter

Immediately, their fear began to melt away. The voice was familiar, and the words reassuring—yet how could it be the Master? Even though he was the Christ, even though he had miraculous abilities, how could he walk upon the stormy sea? There they were, tossed about in their boat and the Lord Jesus was standing a short distance off, unfazed by the storm. Peter had to test the words of this figure—was it really Jesus?

> "And Peter answered him and said, Lord, if it be thou, bid me to come unto thee on the water."
> Matthew 14:28

Peter had an idea. In order to see if it really was the Lord Jesus, he would ask the Master to also empower him to walk upon the sea. If the figure could do so, then it would be the Lord. Peter called out "Lord, if it be thou, bid me to come unto thee on the water…"

It seems as though this was the exact type of reaction that Jesus sought. Not only had the disciples indicated their need for him—they actually asked to come to him. Truly, they had recognized their dependence upon him. Though they may have been frustrated when they jettisoned from the shore earlier that evening, they still recognized that it was imperative for them to follow the Master.

> "And he said, Come. And when Peter was come down out of the ship, he walked on the water, to go to Jesus." Matthew 14:29

Peter went over to one side of the boat and threw his legs over—now he was sitting on the side of the ship. Just try to imagine what would have gone through his mind at this point. Tentatively he put one of his feet down upon the water—and amazingly, he felt firm ground beneath him. He could do this too—the Lord was lifting him up! He stuck the other foot down on the sea, and pushed himself upright off of the boat. Step by step he began to come nearer to the Lord Jesus.

This was unbelievable! Who in all of history had ever done anything like this?! He was standing on top of water. All of his life as a fisherman he spent his time on the sea, yet this was completely out of the realm of his experience. He put one foot down over the other and his Master became closer and closer.

Yet the waves were crashing down around him and the wind was howling by his face. Perhaps one wave fell right next to the disciple and this caused him to take his eyes off of his Lord. He began to notice the mighty waves all around him and began to feel the wind. He probably remembered the extreme danger that he and the others had been in while they were in the boat—they didn't know how they would make it through the storm. Yet now he was there, standing by himself upon the water! If they were in danger on the boat, surely he was in even greater danger by walking on his own upon the water.

Walking on Water

Panic started to set in. How would he survive? The waves were too large for him, the wind was too strong. With each step he took, he noticed that he was starting to sink. As each second past he was lower and lower into the water—what would he do? Truly, he was an excellent swimmer (John 21:7), but no one could swim in this type of storm. If he went down under the waves, he had no hope of survival.

> "But when he saw the wind boisterous, he was afraid; and beginning to sink, he cried, saying, Lord, save me." Matthew 14:30

Fearing for his life and beginning to sink, Peter cried out to the Lord Jesus Christ.

> "And immediately Jesus stretched forth his hand, and caught him, and said unto him, O thou of little faith, wherefore didst thou doubt?" Matthew 14:31

Immediately. There was no hesitation, the Lord reached forth his hand and caught Peter, lifting him up once again. One can only imagine the relief that spread over the disciple's face and he was pulled up from the sea and stood upon the water again with his Master. The slight rebuke would remind him of the need for focus—his eyes must always remain upon Christ. He could not allow himself to get distracted by everything around. His eyes must remain fixed—we do well to heed the same lesson. When we start to think upon the waves and the wind which storm around us, we begin to take our eyes off of the Lord, and we begin to sink. Let us look to Jesus, the author and finisher of faith and we will be given strength to finish the course.

Nevertheless, once Peter stumbled and gave in to his distractions, when he cried out to Jesus, the Lord was there—immediately. The Lord came to him and saved him from the storm. Now, he was with Jesus—and there was no other place that he would rather be (Luke 22:33, John 21:7).

So thankful for his Master, the two of them walked together back to the boat.

Christ in the Boat

> "And when they were come into the ship, the wind ceased." Matthew 14:32

Once the two of them entered back into the boat, the wind ceased. The storm subsided. The waves calmed, the wind stopped, and the sea was still. It was incredible. This was now the second time in which the disciples had seen the Lord's power over the sea. No man could do things like this. Never before had they seen someone walk upon the water.

> "Then they that were in the ship came and worshipped him, saying, Of a truth thou art the Son of God." Matthew 14:33

What other reaction could they have? What would you have done? The only appropriate thing to do was to fall at the foot of this man, recognizing the greatness of his Father and acknowledging his sonship. This was what was deserved! The disciples forgot their worries, abandoned their frustration, and fell down at the feet of the Son of God—in awe. May we have the same response.

> "Then they <u>willingly</u> received him into the ship: and immediately the ship was at the land whither they went." John 6:21

Before the events took place during these early morning hours, this verse may not have been possible. Perhaps the disciples would *not* have *willingly* received Christ into the boat—perhaps they would have wondered about his Messiahship, since he rejected the crown from the multitude. Yet he had reassured them by affirming that he was truly the Christ, and he had demonstrated his power over the elements. He had walked upon the sea and calmed the storm. Truly, he was the Son of God. Truly, they were his disciples, and they would follow him—even if they didn't understand all of the reasons for his actions.

Upon settling into the boat, immediately the ship reached Capernaum where the disciples were headed. As soon as they received Christ into the boat, they reached their destination. After all of their toil, the night was well nigh over and the day had come.

The Parable

Such was the story of the walking upon the water. It is a story of victory, as we experience the trial of the Lord when facing the crowds who wanted to make him king. It is a story of empathy, as we see the disciples struggling to understand their Master's actions and as we see their frustration as they watched their hopes fall to the ground. Yet it is also a story of encouragement as we watch the Lord Jesus Christ come to the rescue of his followers in their time of agony and weakness.

The parable that is beneath this story is similarly exciting and dramatic, but with a special twist. This parable includes both you and me. Working off of the parable which began at the feeding of the five thousand—which showed the sacrifice of Christ and the gathering together of his disciples after the resurrection—this parable begins with Jesus' ascension to heaven and shows the toil of his disciples as they wait for him to return.

Again, just as with the feeding of the five thousand, the exposition of the parable is taken from the gospel of John—he specifically chose to mention certain things and specifically chose to leave out others for the purpose of showing the parable.

Up a Mountain

The parable begins with the Lord Jesus Christ ascending up into a mountain, while his disciples stayed down below:

> "When Jesus therefore perceived that they would come and take him by force, to make him a king, he departed again into a mountain himself alone. And when even was now come, his disciples went down unto the sea." John 6:15-16

The Lord went up and the disciples stayed down—a remarkable parallel to his ascension into heaven. This was something in which the disciples could not follow him. They had to remain behind, and in remaining behind, they went out onto the sea.

Sea of Galilee

> "And entered into a ship, and went over the sea toward Capernaum. And it was now dark, and Jesus was not come to them." John 6:17

Their Lord had gone and the disciples were alone upon the sea. Darkness settled upon the land. In terms of the parable, the Lord had just ascended up to heaven and the disciples were now on their own. They had been sent out onto the sea, which Scripturally is often used to represent the nations:

> "But <u>the wicked are like the troubled sea</u>, when it cannot rest, whose waters cast up mire and dirt." Isaiah 57:20

The sea is equated to the wicked, or the people of the world. Again, this same definition is given to the symbol in the book of Revelation.

> "And he saith unto me, The waters which thou sawest, where the whore sitteth, are peoples, and multitudes, and nations, and tongues." Revelation 17:15

The sea is representative of the nations—hence why John referred to it as the "sea of Tiberias," rather than the "sea of Galilee," because Tiberias was the emperor of the Roman world at that time (John 6:1). He was seeking to get his readers to see the connection between the sea and the world. The Lord had ascended to heaven and his disciples were out upon the sea—they had been sent out into the nations. Their job was to go among the people of the world and be a light—as it said in John's gospel, "it was now dark."

After Jesus went up to heaven, darkness came upon the face of the earth. The light of the world had departed (John 8:12, John 9:5), leaving behind communities which were full of shadows and wickedness. The world was enveloped in darkness—spiritual darkness. In a prophecy of the age just before the establishment of the Kingdom, the prophet Isaiah wrote of the spiritual darkness of the world:

> "Arise, shine; for thy light is come, and the glory of the LORD is risen upon thee. For, behold, <u>the darkness shall cover the earth, and gross darkness the people</u>: for the LORD shall arise upon thee, and his glory shall be seen upon thee." Isaiah 60:1-2

During the period in which Christ is absent from this world, the earth is shrouded in darkness. He was the light and the light is gone. For the time being, the disciples must each seek to be their own individual lights—until the day when the light of the world returns. This is actually what the disciples were looking for as they rowed upon the sea of Tiberias—"And it was now dark, and Jesus was not come to them."

The disciples were waiting for the Lord to come—much like us today. They were waiting for him—and as they were waiting, they were in a boat. Typically in Scripture, a boat is used as a symbol for the ecclesia! Notice that when the flood came upon the earth, it was only the people who were in the ark that were saved!

> "And every living substance was destroyed which was upon the face of the ground, both man, and cattle,

and the creeping things, and the fowl of the heaven; and they were destroyed from the earth: <u>and Noah only remained alive, and they that were with him in the ark.</u>" Genesis 7:23

Every living thing was destroyed from off of the earth—all except for the animals and people that were in the ark. Those who had been separated for God were the ones who were saved. Within the ark was a community of those who were set apart—representative of a body of believers, the ecclesia. Within this parable, the boat represents the ecclesia of God—and that was possibly the reason that John didn't mention anything about Peter getting out of the boat and walking upon the water. This wouldn't fit at all with the parable—the apostle didn't want to encourage anyone to walk away from the ecclesia!

Start to put this parable together. The Master has ascended to heaven. His disciples are down below on earth and they have been sent out into the dark world, yet they are not completely on their own. They have one another. They are together as the body of Christ, and together they are waiting for their king to come, but he has not yet shown himself. Still they wait, looking for him. As they wait, they continue to head towards their final destination—Capernaum (John 6:17).

"Capernaum" means "city of comfort." In the gospel of Matthew it is described as Christ's city:

> "And he entered into a ship, and passed over, and <u>came into his own city</u>. And, behold, they brought to him a man sick of the palsy, lying on a bed: and Jesus seeing their faith said unto the sick of the palsy; Son,

be of good cheer; thy sins be forgiven thee."
Matthew 9:1

Mark recorded this exact same miracle, and he wrote that the event took place in Capernaum (Mark 2:1-5). Thus, Capernaum is the city of comfort and the Lord's own city—an apt description of a place which represents the Kingdom of God. Capernaum is the final destination of the disciples and represents the final destination of all of Christ's followers. All throughout this event, this was where the twelve were headed.

The Storm

While they were sailing towards Capernaum, they ran into difficulties—a huge storm appeared.

> "And the sea arose by reason of a great wind that blew." John 6:18

A storm had come. A great wind began to blow against them and against their little boat. It was the wind which caused the storm and which created the waves. The wind was behind the mighty trial which came upon the disciples—it whipped up the sea until the waves tossed the boat to and fro.

> "That we henceforth be no more children, tossed to and fro, and carried about with every <u>wind of doctrine</u>, by the sleight of men, and cunning craftiness, whereby they lie in wait to deceive." Ephesians 4:14

The wind represents the doctrines of men. It is some type of false teaching. This teaching swiftly caresses the waters until it stirs them up. The teaching of the world blew back and forth over the nations until it made the people drunk with its ideas. These ideas were so persuasive and so enticing that even members of the ecclesia became deluded by them and soon the ecclesial boat finds itself in turmoil. There are members who are clinging to this doctrine and other members who stand firm upon the faith once delivered to the saints. The winds of doctrine blow the boat about.

This is what is illustrated by this parable. The disciples had separated from the Lord, they were now in the darkness of the world seeking to reach the other side of the sea. They were together in an ecclesia. Yet soon, troubles arose. Soon, false ideas began to propagate until the ecclesia found itself being tossed about by various winds of doctrine. This was exactly the state of the ecclesia in the first century:

> "For I know this, that after my departing shall grievous wolves enter in among you, not sparing the flock. Also of your own selves shall men arise, speaking perverse things, to draw away disciples after them." Acts 20:29-30

Paul prophesied that people would enter into the ecclesia at Ephesus and they would cause problems. They would teach false doctrines and teach ideas of the world. This came to pass just as it was foretold—and only a few years later.

> "Unto the angel of the ecclesia of Ephesus write; These things saith he that holdeth the seven stars in his right hand, who walketh in the midst of the seven golden candlesticks; I know thy works, and thy labor, and thy patience, and how thou canst not bear

them which are evil: and <u>thou hast tried them which say they are apostles, and are not, and hast found them liars.</u>" Revelation 2:1-2

When speaking to the ecclesia in Ephesus around AD 96, the Lord Jesus recognized that this ecclesia had been contending for the Truth. The issues of which Paul prophesied had come to pass. There were those in their ecclesia who falsely acted as apostles and sought to teach false ideas. Throughout the first century and all of the centuries which ensued—even today—this has still been a major issue which has plagued Christ's ecclesia. Because various members of the body do not have a strong enough knowledge of the Truth and a good enough foundation in Scripture, they are blown about by every wind of doctrine and in turn, the ecclesia is tossed to and fro.

Sadly, the storm didn't cease *until* the Lord entered the boat—that is to say that the false ideas that wreck havoc in the ecclesia will not cease until the Lord Jesus himself has put an end to them. The false doctrines which have been brought in today through the spirit of humanism are just part of the overall storm of falsehood which will continue to batter our community until the Lord returns. We must examine our own beliefs to make sure that we do not carry any of these damaging and unscriptural ideas, and just like the apostles, keep rowing—keep contending against the storm.

> "So when they had rowed about five and twenty or thirty furlongs, they see Jesus walking on the sea, and drawing nigh unto the ship: and they were afraid." John 6:19

Walking on Water

In the midst of the sea, the Lord appeared to them—take note of their reaction. They were afraid—but his voice brought them comfort. May it be that the voice of the Lord brings comfort to us as well at his coming.

> "But he saith unto them, It is I; be not afraid. Then they willingly received him into the ship: and immediately the ship was at the land whither they went." John 6:20-21

Once the Lord had come into the boat, they were immediately at Capernaum—the city of comfort. They had reached the Kingdom of God. Their Lord was with them and they were at his city. At one point, they may have given up hope that they would ever make it to the other side. They may have looked around themselves, seen their boat thrown about on the waves, seen how far they were from any land whatsoever, and wanted to give up hope. Yet they didn't. They kept rowing all throughout the night—and as the day began to dawn, the Lord appeared to them and soon they reached Capernaum. Let us keep this in mind whenever we feel as though the struggle against sin and against falsehood is too difficult. Stay in the boat. Keep rowing. The Lord will come soon.

> "And that, knowing the time, that now it is high time to awake out of sleep: for now is our salvation nearer than when we believed. <u>The night is far spent, the day is at hand</u>: let us therefore cast off the works of darkness, and let us put on the armor of light." Romans 13:11-12

The day is near—just as Christ came to the disciples and saved them from the storm, so will our Messiah come. The parallels between this event and the struggles of the disciples of Christ throughout all ages are unmistakable. When this parable is put together with the parable of the feeding of the five thousand, a beautiful picture unfolds:

- The sacrifice of Christ took place upon the mountain and the bread of life was distributed to a multitude
- The twelve were gathered back together so that none might be lost
- The Jews, based upon their misunderstanding of God's plan and His will, begin to cause problems
- Meanwhile, Christ ascended up to heaven and his disciples embarked upon a voyage across the sea of nations to the city of comfort
- On their journey the ecclesia was blown about by the winds of doctrine—it almost seemed as though there would be no end to the storm, yet the winds ceased when the Lord Jesus Christ came to them
- Once Christ had come to them, they were immediately at the city of comfort

The parable is one which gives us encouragement and one which reminds us to stand fast during trying times. Just as the disciples, we wait for the Lord. Just as the disciples, we will one day see him—and just as the disciples, by the grace of God, we too will stand in the Lord's city.

Even so, come, Lord Jesus.

Amen.

Chapter 6
The Man Born Blind

Much time had passed since Christ walked upon the water. Passover had come and gone, so had the feast of Pentecost, and even the feast of tabernacles (John 7:2). The time for the Lord's sacrifice was drawing closer and closer—now it was only a few months away. It was probably around this time—a little bit after the feast of tabernacles—that the Lord Jesus and his disciples passed by a man who had been born blind.

> "And as Jesus passed by, he saw a man which was blind from his birth." John 9:1

Jesus was "passing by." This phrase links the events of John 9 back to the events of the previous chapter. The Lord had been preaching to the Jews about the freedom and the liberty that he could give to them—when a dispute arose about the greatness of Abraham compared to the greatness of Jesus. The Lord ended his remarks by saying, "Before Abraham was, I am," meaning that he was the Christ. Before Abraham was even born, the Lord Jesus had been chosen to be the Messiah. Upon this remark, the Jews picked up stones to throw at the Master.

> "Then took they up stones to cast at him: but Jesus hid himself, and went out of the temple, going through the midst of them, and so <u>passed by</u>." John 8:59

Thus, here is the connection with the story of the man born blind. Jesus left the temple and "passed by." While he was passing by, he came upon a man who was blind from birth. It appears as though the Lord hadn't planned on saying anything to him—and the man didn't say anything to Christ. The Master was simply going to pass by and be on his way. However, when the disciples saw the man, they had a burning question which they had to ask the Teacher:

> "And his disciples asked him, saying, Master, who did sin, this man, or his parents, that he was born blind?" John 9:2

Throughout the ages, disease and sickness were always associated with sin (John 9:34). It was understood that the diseased were cursed by God—because they were so direly afflicted, their sorrow and suffering must have been a punishment from above. At times, this attribution was true, but not always. The story of Job is full proof of that; Job was a righteous man, yet he shared in an immense amount of suffering and sickness. Nevertheless, this idea still prevailed at the time of the Lord Jesus Christ. If someone was sick or diseased, it was believed that they were a sinner, cursed by God for their sins.

As is the case with most false doctrines, there are consequences of them that simply do not make sense. The blindness of this man was exactly one of those consequences—and thus the disciples asked the Lord about him. Typically it was thought that people were punished by disease because of their *own sins*. But this man didn't seem to entirely fit with that idea—how could a man who was blind from *birth* have done anything to bring that blindness upon himself? This was

The Man Born Blind

the issue upon which the disciples had stumbled. It was utterly impossible for a man *born blind* to have committed a sin—therefore, why was he blind? Perhaps it was because of his parents—could they have been the sinners?

The Lord was petitioned to explain this dilemma—and how his explanation would have puzzled the disciples! According to the Master, this man didn't sin; the disciples had judged rightly in that matter. Yet, his parents had not sinned either—and that was the catch. The disciples' understanding wasn't quite right, it was missing something. This man didn't sin and neither did his parents. Rather, this blindness had come on him for the glory of God.

Now, pause the story here and begin to listen to this story through the ears of the blind man—a discussion has just commenced in front of you. It's a discussion which isn't altogether unfamiliar, you've heard it before—people seeking to determine how it was that you were blind. Was it through something that you did, or something that your parents had done? Once again, people have stopped and discussed this in front of you—staring at you, the sinner. All of your life you've been a beggar—you've never been able to do anything else. People say that you've been cursed by God, some feel sorry for you, but others seem to think that you somehow brought this blindness upon yourself. For years, you've had to have your parents, maybe your neighbors, lead you to this begging spot each day. And now, probably not for the first time, people have come to you to discuss whose sin brought your affliction into your life.

Expecting to hear the same debate as you have heard so many times in the past, you keep up your begging. But then another man begins to speak, and his voice resounds with authority. You've never heard anyone speak like this man before—"Neither hath this man sinned, nor his parents: but that the works of God should be made manifest in him."

Those words make you freeze. This was a man who actually took the blame off of you, who said that you weren't a cursed sinner, but who actually said that this blindness came upon you for the glory of God. The glory of God! What could that mean? How could blindness ever possibly show God's glory? Who was this man and what did he mean? As you're thinking about those things, he continues his remarks:

> "I must work the works of him that sent me, while it is day: the night cometh, when no man can work. As long as I am in the world, I am the light of the world." John 9:4-5

He said that he was the "light of the world." Again, another statement that demanded more explanation—what did he mean? You pause. Standing before you is a man who said that your blindness would be used for God's honor, and who just claimed to be the light of the world. Is it possible that the man in front of you is a prophet? Your heart starts to beat faster and you feel a bit of nervous energy. Perhaps it's true—you could be face to face with a prophet. As you're thinking these thoughts, you hear him spit on the ground and mix the dirt with his spittle.

Unexpectedly, you wince as you feel him spreading dirt all over your eyes. What is he doing? Is the prophet

The Man Born Blind

going to use you for one of his signs? What did he mean about being the light of the world? Why is he touching you? Could it be that you might receive your sight? Maybe...

"Go, wash in the pool of Siloam."

And that's all he says. Nothing else is spoken and nothing else is done. You pause for a brief second—you're near the temple, and the pool of Siloam is all the way at the south side of the city. It isn't a short walk...how will you get there? On top of that, the man never explained why you were supposed to go to the pool. But you'd never heard anyone speak like him.

You jump up and feverishly feel your way through the city.

Just imagine how the blind man would have felt throughout this entire experience. His natural urge would have been to peel the clay off of his eyes. There were probably onlookers who mocked him as he fumbled his way through town with mud on his face. Yet, despite the mocking and the jesting, he continued on in faith. He had been touched by Christ, a man unlike any he had ever known, and he had to continue.

Eventually he reached the pool—probably splashing into it with relief. He had finally made it. Others likely stared at him as he joyfully threw water into his face, rinsing the dirt and clay off. As he opened his eyes, for the first time in his life, he could see.

He could see the water in which he was standing. He could see his neighbors and he could see his parents. What a beautiful thing had happened to him! The prophet had anointed his eyes with clay, he had endured the walk through the city, had splashed the water onto his face, and now he could see!

But there was a caveat. The day on which he had been healed was a sabbath—and all because of that, he would be let down by everyone whom he trusted. As the story progresses, he will be let down by his neighbors, by his own family, and even by the religious shepherds.

His Neighbors

It was probably when the man born blind returned to where he used to beg that his neighbors realized that there was something different about him. Now, he was looking at things, he was studying them, as though he could actually see what it was that he was observing:

> "The neighbors therefore, and they which before had seen him that was blind, said, Is not this he that sat and begged? Some said, This is he: others said, He is like him: but he said, I am he." John 9:8-9

Upon seeing this man, the neighbors disputed with one another—was this the man? How was it then that he appeared to be able to see? Yet the man born blind confirmed that he truly was the one who had been the beggar.

> "Therefore said they unto him, How were thine eyes opened? He answered and said, A man that is called Jesus made clay, and anointed mine eyes, and said unto me, Go to the pool of Siloam, and wash: and I went and washed, and I received sight." John 9:10-12

The Man Born Blind

After hearing that he was the man who had sat and begged, the neighbors immediately wanted to know how it was that he could see—no one had ever heard of anything happening like this before! A man who was blind from birth had always stayed a man who was blind—never had a man like this been given sight (John 9:32). Thus the blind man reiterated his story, but there was now a blemish in the excitement. This was now the second time (in John's record) in which the Lord had healed on a Sabbath. He had not stopped—back when he healed the man at the pool of Bethesda, the authorities had sought to kill him for it. Now, the offenses had continued, and the man born blind would be taken by his neighbors to testify of the Lord Jesus before the religious council.

There he stood, betrayed by his neighbors, looking at a group of the Pharisees. First, they asked him how it was that he could now see.

> "Then again the Pharisees also asked him how he had received his sight. He said unto them, He put clay upon mine eyes, and I washed, and do see." John 9:15

He told them his story. The Lord put clay upon his eyes, he washed the clay off, and then he could see. The testimony was simple—it was far from being a complicated matter. Yet somehow these words provoked an argument amidst this council of Pharisees—and how astounded this man would have been as he listened to them debate! These men were supposed to be the most knowledgeable people in the nation, they were supposed to have the most acute understanding of God's ways, and yet they were put to confusion over what had just happened! They began to argue right in front of the man!

> "Therefore said some of the Pharisees, This man is not of God, because he keepeth not the sabbath day. Others said, How can a man that is a sinner do such miracles? And there was a division among them." John 9:16

The man would probably look back and forth as each side passionately said their view of the matter. Yet the spectacle was not over—after debating the issue, the Pharisees were not able to reach a conclusion. In hopes of settling the dispute, they actually turned to the man and asked him what *he* thought! Imagine the scenario! Again, these were the men who were supposed to be *his* teachers—these were the men who were supposed to bring the law to the people. Now, they turned to him for an answer. The man would have been taken aback, suddenly beginning to realize that the trust which the religious leaders received from the people was not entirely warranted. Nevertheless, the man firmly proclaimed his belief in the Master:

> "They say unto the blind man again, What sayest thou of him, that he hath opened thine eyes? He said, He is a prophet." John 9:17

The confession signifies the growth of the man's faith. He may have toyed with the idea that the Lord Jesus was a prophet before this, yet when speaking to others, he never called him such previously—before, Christ was simply "a man that is called Jesus" (John 9:11). Now, in the man's eyes, "he is a prophet." His faith was beginning to grow—unfortunately, the same could not

The Man Born Blind

be said for the faith of the Jews. Though they heard the testimony of the man, they refused to believe.

His Parents

> "But the Jews did not believe concerning him, that he had been blind, and received his sight, until they called the parents of him that had received his sight." John 9:18

Even though the man witnessed to his view of the Lord Jesus, the Jews characteristically refused to believe. To add to this, not only did they stay in unbelief, but they sought to prove the man wrong. Since they couldn't come to a decision on their own about Jesus, the Pharisees chose another tactic—instead of trying to malign the reputation of Christ, they would simply prove that a miracle had never actually taken place. They would call in his parents and prove that he have never truly been blind! The Pharisees rejected the man's testimony and now they in fact sought to prove him a liar. Thus, the man born blind had been let down by his neighbors and let down by the religious leaders. Soon, his parents would follow the same pattern:

> "And they asked them, saying, Is this your son, who ye say was born blind? how then doth he now see? His parents answered them and said, We know that this is our son, and that he was born blind: But by what means he now seeth, we know not; or who hath opened his eyes, we know not: he is of age; ask him: he shall speak for himself." John 9:19-21

As they stood before the council, his parents refused to stand by him. Truly, they admitted that he was their son—which foiled the Pharisees plans—but they couldn't admit how it was that he could see. Fear had overtaken them. Unlike their son, who boldly proclaimed that he believed Jesus of Nazareth to be a prophet, his parents let him down and professed that they knew not how he could now see—and now the man had been let down by his parents. This was the first time in which he had *ever* seen them in his life, and they refused to give him their support. Thus the man had been betrayed by his neighbors, betrayed by the religious rulers, and betrayed by his family.

The Pharisees

At this point, the Pharisees were beginning to get desperate. It was clear that this man had once been blind and that he could now see—it was undeniable that a mighty miracle had taken place. Yet how could that be? How could a man who had the power of God break the Sabbath law? It didn't seem to make sense to them. Regardless of the miracle, they believed that no one sent from God could break the laws in that way—therefore, Christ must be a sinner. As a result of this feeling, they turned their attention again to the man, deciding that they would no longer look for evidence, but that they would instead seek to pressure and verbally intimidate him until he admitted that Christ was a sinner:

> "Then again called they the man that was blind, and said unto him, <u>Give God the praise</u>: we know that this man is a sinner." John 9:24

This phrase, "Give God the praise," is actually a quote of the Old Testament, although it may not first seem that way. In some of the more literal translations, this phrase is rendered as "Give glory to God."

> "Then a second time they called the man who was blind, and they said to him, <u>Give glory to God</u>. We know that this man is a sinner." John 9:24 LITV

> "They called, therefore, a second time the man who was blind, and they said to him, '<u>Give glory to God</u>, we have known that this man is a sinner.'" John 9:24 YLT

"Give glory to God!" This was a direct allusion from the Old Testament by these Pharisees. They were hearkening back to the story of Joshua, to a time when one man had used deceit and his deceit had resulted in the death of 36 men.

> "And Joshua said unto Achan, My son, <u>give, I pray thee, glory to the LORD God of Israel</u>, and make confession unto him; and tell me now what thou hast done; hide it not from me." Joshua 7:19

This was the same phrase! At this time in Joshua, the forces of Israel had gone to fight against Ai—yet they had lost the battle. Something had gone wrong—Yahweh was to fight for them, but He didn't in this first battle. Why? The reason was that one man had taken from Jericho some of the devoted things. The spoils of Jericho were supposed to be devoted to God, yet this man, Achan, had taken them. They were hidden in his tent, and he had deceived the rest of the nation, seeking to hide these items from them. Yet his deceit could not be concealed.

This was the situation that these Pharisees paralleled with the situation before them! Here they were, righteous leaders (in their eyes!) like Joshua, looking at a man full of deceit. "Give God the glory," they said. "We know that this man is a sinner." It was almost as though they were telling the man born blind that he needed to stop being like Achan—he needed to stop living in deceit! Just as Achan to Joshua, the man born blind needed to admit his lie. The Pharisees were now using intimation against the man!

Despite the powerful indictment against the man born blind, he was not moved. Instead, he stood upon the simple truth: "I was blind, and now I can see."

What a contrast his declaration was to the twisted accusation of the Pharisees—so often this is the case. The Truth is plain and simple, and yet the mighty churches of the world will twist and wrest Scripture to somehow make it conform to their ideas. May we examine ourselves to see that we are consistently standing upon the simple and logical Truth. It may not always be pleasant, as can be seen from the story of this man, yet the end of the matter always works out for good.

With each response from the man, the Pharisees would have become more and more frustrated—they couldn't disprove the miracle, and now they couldn't seem to intimidate the man into calling Christ a sinner. Finally, not knowing what else to do, they decided to reexamine the story. They asked him again to tell them what had happened:

> "Then said they to him again, What did he to thee? how opened he thine eyes?" John 9:26

The Man Born Blind

These Pharisees were stuck in their traditions and rituals—they didn't truly want to listen to the man at all! If they had wanted to listen, they would have heard him the first time and they wouldn't have sought to intimidate him. It was clear to the man that they weren't interested in following Christ—all they wanted was to condemn him. Thus, through mockery, he exposed their intent:

> "He answered them, I have told you already, and ye did not hear: wherefore would ye hear it again? will ye also be his disciples?" John 9:27

Based off of what this man had experienced with them, it was obvious that the Pharisees did not want to be Christ's disciples—but that was precisely why the man said it. He was tired of this foolishness and he knew that they would not change! As a contrast to them and their lack of faith, his faith had actually grown all throughout this account. Previously he had said that the Lord was a prophet—now he claimed to be Christ's disciple—"will ye *also* be his disciples?" This declaration was met with contempt.

> "Then they reviled him, and said, Thou art his disciple; but we are Moses' disciples. We know that God spake unto Moses: as for this fellow, we know not from whence he is." John 9:28

It was almost as though the man's response set the Pharisees into a frenzy—they were burning with anger for him. His insolence towards them was unbearable. He might have been a follower of Jesus, but truly they followed Moses. They knew that God spoke to Moses, but they couldn't tell anything about Jesus—he performed miracles, but he broke their understanding of the law. The man born blind heard these words and answered them confidently and powerfully:

> "Why herein is a marvellous thing, that ye know not from whence he is, and yet he hath opened mine eyes. Now we know that God heareth not sinners: but if any man be a worshipper of God, and doeth his will, him he heareth. Since the world began was it not heard that any man opened the eyes of one that was born blind. If this man were not of God, he could do nothing." John 9:30

This reply was intolerable. Again he sought to correct them and they wouldn't hear it. This man was born in sin—he was diseased. How could he possibly try to teach them, the *righteous?* They were favored by God, he was a sinner. He needed to learn his place and learn respect. Until then, they did not want to have anything to do with him, and thus they cast him out of the synagogue—hoping that he would recognize the error of his ways.

> "They answered and said unto him, Thou wast altogether born in sins, and dost thou teach us? And they cast him out." John 9:34

This man with budding faith had just been rejected by his own religion. He had been forsaken by his neighbors, disappointed by his parents, and thrown out by the religious rulers. Yet though he had been cast off by all whom may have cared for him before, he had not been cast off by the Lord Jesus. Christ was unlike any other man to him. The Lord would stand by him. Where all men saw him as a sinner and left his side, the

Lord came to him to give him hope. He would appear to give the man encouragement and strength.

Telling the Parable

The story of the man born blind is an amazing picture of the conversion of one man. Yet hidden within this story is the conversion of a multitude.

As mentioned earlier, this event is tied to the last few verses of the previous chapter in John. In those verses, Christ had just been "stoned," but didn't actually die—ie, the people sought to kill him, but he evaded from their presence. After that, he was in the story for a little while longer, but soon disappeared (John 9:12). He healed the man, and then he was gone. The time in which this took place was a sabbath—the time in which the Jews enforced their rules.

This is the setting of the parable—in those preceding events, the parable shows the death and resurrection of Christ and then his ascension to heaven, when he was no longer in the world. The exact time is shown by the fact that it is a sabbath day; this is the time in which the Jews still have a measure of power, when they can enforce their laws and regulations—it is the time before AD 70. This setting is exactly the same as the period shown by the parable of the invalid. The Lord Jesus had ascended to heaven and it was the time of Jewish power before their downfall.

Identifying the Man Born Blind

Just as with the parable of the invalid, the man born blind also represents a group of people—although he is quite a different group. Whereas the man at the pool of Bethesda didn't seem to have a very keen interest in being healed, this man was willing to walk all the way to the pool of Siloam with mud on his eyes. Whereas the invalid gave in to the Jews and sought to please them, the man born blind stood up to their false ideas and criticized them. The two men are almost complete contrasts! Immediately then, it should be realized that it is doubtful that the man born blind represents the Jews—as did the invalid. This conclusion is supported by the fact that the man born blind was *healed from blindness*. This does not fit with the Jews at all—almost every time that the New Testament refers to those who *were not* healed of their blindness, it is referring to the Jews. When the Lord Jesus came to heal them, many of them wanted to stay blind, or like the invalid, they were healed for a time and then went back to their traditions:

> "But though he had done so many miracles before them, yet they believed not on him: that the saying of Esaias the prophet might be fulfilled, which he spake, Lord, who hath believed our report? and to whom hath the arm of the LORD been revealed? Therefore they could not believe, because that Esaias said again, He hath blinded their eyes, and hardened their heart; that they should not see with their eyes, nor understand with their heart, and be converted, and I should heal them." John 12:37-40

The Jews didn't want to see and as a result, they were made blind—the complete opposite of the man in this parable! Because of their stubbornness, God temporarily closed their eyes. Jesus emphasized the same thing just after the parable of the sower.

The Man Born Blind

> "For this people's heart is waxed gross, and their ears are dull of hearing, and <u>their eyes they have closed</u>; lest at any time they should see with their eyes and hear with their ears, and should understand with their heart, and should be converted, and I should heal them." Matthew 13:15

The Jews had closed their eyes! They had come to a point in which they did not want to see the Truth. Their rituals became more important to them than the true message of the law—and because they closed their eyes, God blinded them. However, this Jewish blindness was not permanent, it would simply continue until a fresh generation decided that they finally wanted to see. But there was also a second reason that the Jews had been blinded—their blindness brought the gospel to another group of people:

> "I say then, Have they stumbled that they should fall? God forbid: but rather <u>through their fall salvation is come unto the Gentiles</u>, for to provoke them to jealousy." Romans 11:11

Through the fall of the Jews, salvation was offered to the Gentiles. Before that time, the saving message had largely only been preached to Jews. It was this blindness which gave the Gentiles an opportunity. The apostle said the same thing again in even more explicit terms:

> "For I would not, brethren, that ye should be ignorant of this mystery, lest ye should be wise in your own conceits; <u>that blindness in part is happened to Israel, until the fulness of the Gentiles be come in</u>." Romans 11:25

The Jews were blinded so that the Gentiles, so that *many of us,* could have an opportunity to open up our eyes to the plan of God—and it is this group that is a likely candidate for the man born blind. It would seem quite odd to have referred to the Jews as "blind from birth"—rather, they would be better described as a man who could see at one point, and then became blind. Yet, when that term is applied to Gentiles, it fits wonderfully. As a whole, in the first century, the Gentiles had never been able to see—they had always been blind. The gospel hadn't been preached to them as it had been to the Jews. This conclusion, that the man born blind represents the Gentiles, is supported by the way in which the Lord Jesus described himself just before healing the man. When he was standing in front of the man born blind, the Lord made a statement about himself:

> "As long as I am in the world, I am the light of the world." John 9:5

Just before the healing of the man born blind, the Master stated that he was the "light of the world." Why was it that the Lord chose to say that about himself at this particular point? He had said it one chapter earlier (John 8:12) and now he said it again. Why did he say it before this particular miracle? Why not say it before the healing of the invalid or before the feeding of the five thousand? Perhaps because the theme of Christ as the light of the world is strongly connected to what this miracle represented—a number of times in Scripture, the Master is described as a "light" to the Gentiles. An example of this can be seen in one of the prophecies of Isaiah, in a section known as the "Servant Songs"—prophecies which would be fully fulfilled by the Messiah:

> "And he said, It is a light thing that thou shouldest be my servant to raise up the tribes of Jacob, and to restore the preserved of Israel: I will also give thee for a <u>light to the Gentiles</u>, that thou mayest be my salvation unto the end of the earth." Isaiah 49:6

The Lord Jesus would not only be sent to raise up the tribes of Jacob and to restore the preserved of Israel, but he would also be a *light* to the Gentiles. Again, this same thing was said by Simeon when he saw the Lord Jesus as an infant:

> "For mine eyes have seen thy salvation, which thou hast prepared before the face of all people; <u>a light to lighten the Gentiles</u>, and the glory of thy people Israel." Luke 2:30-32

These were the words proclaimed by Simeon while Christ was in the temple. The apostle Paul said the same thing of him when speaking before Agrippa:

> "That Christ should suffer, and that he should be the first that should rise from the dead, and <u>should shew light unto the people, and to the Gentiles</u>." Acts 26:23

Multiple times in Scripture, the Lord Jesus is called a light to the Gentiles, or something similar. Yet the connection between the healing of the man born blind and the gospel being preached to the Gentiles is even stronger. Not only is there a link between Christ being a light and the Word being preached to the Gentiles, but there is also a connection to healing those who were blind. In another of the "Servant Songs," the prophet Isaiah wrote of the Messiah:

> "I the LORD have called thee in righteousness, and will hold thine hand, and will keep thee, and give thee for a covenant of the people, for a <u>light of the Gentiles; to open the blind eyes</u>, to bring out the prisoners the prison, and them that sit in darkness out of the prison house." Isaiah 42:6-7

The Messiah would be a light to the Gentiles—*and* he would open the blind eyes. This is exactly what was shown in the parable. The Lord Jesus, as the light of the world healed the blind eyes and brought that true light to the Gentiles. Again, these same type of words were used by the apostle Paul. He was commanded by God to open the eyes of the Gentiles, and turn them to the light:

> "Delivering thee from the people, and from the Gentiles, unto whom now I send thee, <u>to open their eyes, and to turn them from darkness to light</u>, and from the power of Satan unto God, that they may receive forgiveness of sins, and inheritance among them which are sanctified by faith that is in me." Acts 26:17-18

The healing of the man born blind was a picture of this—it was a picture of the Gentiles having their eyes opened and being able to see the light of the world. That's the reason that the Master called himself the "light of the world" just before the man was healed! He was connecting this man to the Gentiles! Putting this together with the setting, the parable is telling a story—the Lord Jesus Christ had been killed and resurrected. Then, he ascended to heaven to be at the right hand of the Father. The Jews were in power and the Gentiles

The Man Born Blind

were given an opportunity to see. But, in order for them to see, they needed to wash the clay off of their eyes.

The Clay

In this story, the clay is representative of the flesh—or human thinking. It is used this way in the book of Isaiah:

> "Woe unto him that striveth with his Maker! let the potsherd strive with the potsherds of the earth. Shall the clay say to him that fashioneth it, What makest thou? or thy work, He hath no hands?" Isaiah 45:9

In this reference, man is referred to as "the clay." Clay represents humanity, or the flesh. Just a few chapters later in Isaiah, this same idea can be seen once more:

> "But now, O LORD, thou art our father; we are the clay, and thou our potter; and we all are the work of thy hand." Isaiah 64:8

We are the clay—the clay represents mankind, or simply humanity. In the parable, the Master spit upon the ground, made clay of the dirt and the spittle and then wiped the clay on the blind man's eyes. In order for him to truly see, this clay had to be taken off—it was clearly a symbolic act on the part of the Lord Jesus, he could have healed the man immediately if he so desired. However, the Lord sought to show the picture. If the Gentiles wanted to be able to see, they had to wash off their flesh—and they couldn't just wash off the clay in any pool of the city. The man was specifically told to go to the pool of Siloam.

Glimpses of the Master
The Pool of Siloam

The miracle would only take place if the man went to this particular pool—he couldn't go to one that was closer or one which suited his fancy. He had to go to the pool of Siloam—because the pool of Siloam represented the only name given under heaven whereby men can be saved. This pool represented the Master. John clearly denoted this when he wrote out the interpretation of the word "Siloam":

> "And said unto him, Go, wash in the pool of Siloam, (<u>which is by interpretation, Sent</u>.) He went his way therefore, and washed, and came seeing." John 9:7

The word "Siloam" means "sent." There is a direct connection here between the meaning of the word and what the Lord had said just a few verses prior. When standing in front of the man born blind he said:

> "I must work the works of him <u>that sent me</u>, while it is day: the night cometh, when no man can work." John 9:4

The Lord Jesus had been "sent" by God. In fact, this is something which the apostle emphasized all throughout his gospel. Over and over it is mentioned that the Lord Jesus was sent by God—much more than all of the other gospels combined.

References to Christ being "sent" by God in John:

1. John 3:17	2. John 3:34	3. John 4:34
4. John 5:23	5. John 5:24	6. John 5:30

The Man Born Blind

7. John 5:36	8. John 5:37	9. John 5:38
10. John 6:29	11. John 6:38	12. John 6:39
13. John 6:40	14. John 6:44	15. John 6:57
16. John 7:16	17. John 7:18	18. John 7:28
19. John 7:29	20. John 7:33	21. John 8:16
22. John 8:18	23. John 8:26	24. John 8:29
25. John 8:42	26. John 9:4	27. John 10:36
28. John 11:42	29. John 12:44	30. John 12:45
31. John 12:49	32. John 13:20	33. John 14:24
34. John 15:21	35. John 16:5	36. John 17:3
37. John 17:18	38. John 17:21	39. John 17:23
40. John 17:25	41. John 20:21	

As it can be seen, John's gospel states 41 times that the Lord Jesus was sent by God. Compare this to the number of times in which it is said in the other gospels put together.

References to Christ being "sent" by God in the other gospels:

1. Matthew 10:40	2. Matthew 15:24	3. Matthew 21:37
4. Mark 9:37	5. Mark 12:6	6. Luke 4:18
7. Luke 4:43	8. Luke 9:48	9. Luke 10:16
10. John 6:29	11. John 6:38	12. John 6:39

Constantly the gospel of John shows Christ being the one sent by God—thus, it is clear that when John purposefully gave his readers the meaning of the word "Siloam," that he was trying to create a connection within their minds. The pool of Siloam represents the Lord Jesus! He was the one sent by God! This is why the man born blind could not go to any other pool—it isn't possible to receive salvation through any other than the Lord (Acts 4:12)! If we desire to be saved, we must come to the feet of the Master in Truth. We cannot follow another gospel (Galatians 1:6-9). There is but one faith (Ephesians 4:5) and we must seek to worship in it—the man could only go to the one pool, regardless of the struggle that it caused. Though there were pools which were closer and which were easier to find, in faith he had to go to the pool which represented the Lord Jesus—the one sent by God.

Thus the picture continues to come together—the Gentiles would come to Christ and be healed. They would leave their foolish traditions, they would say "surely our fathers have inherited lies," and they would come to the light of Truth. Their old man of the flesh would be washed through the Lord Jesus Christ, and eventually they would be able to see him. Yet their conversion would not be easy, just as the healing and conversion of the man born blind was not easy. In the first century, after the nations began to learn the Truth, there were a group of people who withstood this "healing" of the Gentiles. There would be people who would try to prevent the apostles from preaching to the Gentiles. This group of people was the Jews, aptly represented by the Pharisees in this parable:

> "And it came to pass in Iconium, that they went both together into the synagogue of the Jews, and so

> spake, that a great multitude both of the Jews and also of the Greeks believed. <u>But the unbelieving Jews stirred up the Gentiles</u>, and made their minds evil affected against the brethren." Acts 14:1-2

When the brethren were preaching in Iconium, the Jews who didn't believe the gospel sought to cause problems—they actually stirred up the Gentiles. Through these efforts, they tried to hinder the preaching of Paul and Barnabas so that the gospel couldn't go out to the nations! The same thing happened just a few chapters later:

> "But when the Jews of Thessalonica had knowledge that the word of God was preached of Paul at Berea, they came thither also, and stirred up the people." Acts 17:13

Throughout the preaching in the first century, the Jews continuously sought to prevent the gospel from being preached. This was exactly what the Pharisees were doing to the man born blind—they tried to hinder his conversion and to prevent him from following the Lord Jesus. Nevertheless, the man born blind stood up to their power and through his belief, he condemned their stubbornness.

Judgment from the Man Born Blind

> "He answered them, I have told you already, <u>and ye did not hear</u>: wherefore would ye hear it again? will ye also be his disciples?" John 9:27

Though he had told them about his healing, the Jews refused to hear. Thus, the man born blind witnessed against them and testified of their hardheartedness. In the same way, the Gentiles, through their belief, witnessed to the unbelief of the Jews:

> "And the next sabbath day came almost the whole city together to hear the word of God. But when the Jews saw the multitudes, they were filled with envy, and spake against those things which were spoken by Paul, contradicting and blaspheming. Then Paul and Barnabas waxed bold, and said, It was necessary that the word of God should first have been spoken to you: <u>but seeing ye put it from you, and judge yourselves unworthy of everlasting life, lo, we turn to the Gentiles</u>. For so hath the Lord commanded us, saying, I have set thee to be a light of the Gentiles, that thou shouldest be for salvation unto the ends of the earth. And when the Gentiles heard this, they were glad, and glorified the word of the Lord: and as many as were ordained to eternal life believed." Acts 13:44-48

The Jews had stayed in unbelief, and as a result, the good news went forth to the Gentiles—because they would listen to it.

> "Be it known therefore unto you, that the salvation of God is sent unto the Gentiles, and <u>that they will hear it</u>." Acts 28:28

Unlike many of the Jews, many of the Gentiles received the word with gladness and excitement. They were willing to hear.

Thus, the parable shows the conversion of the Gentiles. It shows the time after Christ's ascension to heaven, when the eyes of the Gentiles were opened. Christ was preached to them—the Truth about him and his second coming, and they receive it with gladness. Through baptism, they joined the ecclesia and held firm in their belief despite efforts by others to tear it down.

Our Open Eyes

In this story of the conversion of one man is the conversion of a multitude. But there is more. The depth of God's word is fascinating—because not only does this incident simply tell the story of one man, or just the story of a multitude—there is one final story involved—our story. For those of us who are Gentiles, we too were born in blindness. We didn't know the Truth, we didn't know the God of Israel, we didn't know His plan, and we didn't know the Scriptures. But our eyes have been opened and our lives have been forever changed. Christ has come to us and given us a way to be healed. We have washed ourselves in him, through baptism. And we too have had to stand upon the simple Truth when others have sought to discredit it. Thanks be to God for allowing us to see. May we fall on our knees in gratitude before Him—just as the man born blind.

Seeing Christ

> "Jesus heard that they had cast him out; and when he had found him, he said unto him, Dost thou believe on the Son of God? He answered and said, Who is he, Lord, that I might believe on him? And Jesus said unto him, Thou hast both seen him, and it is he that talketh with thee. And he said, Lord, I believe. And he worshipped him." John 9:35-38

Glimpses of the Master

When the Lord heard that the man had been cast out of the synagogue, he came to him and asked him if he believed on the Son of God—this was where the man's faith came to full bloom. In the beginning he saw the Lord Jesus as simply a man, then later a prophet, and now, finally, he prostrated himself before the Master, worshipping him as the Son of God. He believed in the Lord Jesus Christ—that's not to say that he didn't believe before, rather, his belief grew stronger. The Master in fact, proved his former belief by what he said to him—"Thou hast both seen him, and it is he that talketh with thee." At first, however, these words might not appear to prove the man's original belief—in fact, they may seem almost backwards. *First* he said that the man had seen him, *then* that it was he who was talking to the man. That isn't the way that this would typically be said, instead, most people probably would have said "you have talked with him before, and now you see him!"—because the man had never literally seen the Lord until this point. He was blind when they first came into contact! But that's not the way that the Lord said it. Along that same line, Christ said that the blind man had *seen* him—ie, he said it as though it was something that happened in the past! Yet before this moment, the blind man had *never* seen Christ before! Or had he?

The man born blind had never literally seen Christ, but he had seen him through his faith. And so it is with us. Just like the man born blind, we have never seen the Lord Jesus—but through our faith we can. We can see the way in which he lived, we can see his love for his God, we can see his compassion towards his followers. Truly, we have seen him with our faith.

Just as it was with the man born blind, one day we will see the Master—and may we too, like this humble man, fall down before the Lord of glory and worship him, the mighty Son of God.

Chapter 7
The Resurrection of Lazarus

The raising of Lazarus was a sign which should have indisputably declared the Lord Jesus Christ to be different than any other man. Resurrection was something which almost never took place. Elijah had raised the dead and so had Elisha—in addition, the Lord had done it twice before with the raising of the widow's son (Luke 7:14-15) and the raising of Jarius' daughter (Luke 8:54-55). Yet this miracle with Lazarus was altogether different than any of those. Never before had one been raised *after* they had begun to see corruption. Never before had one been raised after lying in the tomb for four days. This miracle should have been positive proof that the Lord Jesus was the Messiah. He was backed by the power of God.

> "There is no man that hath power over the spirit to retain the spirit; neither hath he power in the day of death: and there is no discharge in that war; neither shall wickedness deliver those that are given to it." Ecclesiastes 8:8

No man has power to retain the spirit of God—their breath goes forth and they return to the earth. No man has power in the day of death—all except the Lord Jesus. Constantly he was and is the exception. He had power over the spirit, he had power over death, and he had power over the grave. This miracle was unlike anything anyone had ever seen and should have proved that he possessed the power of God (John 20:31). Yet sadly, for many people it didn't. For many of the Jewish rulers, even the resurrection from the dead could not break through their stony hearts. They refused to turn and they refused to follow Christ. Instead, they became even more zealous about destroying the Lord, and it was this sign which eventually led to his death.

As we examine the story of Lazarus' resurrection, may we be deeply moved by the way in which the Lord works with his followers. He does not leave them and he does not forsake them (Hebrews 13:5). He empathizes with their grief and weeps alongside them—just as he did with Mary and Martha. He isn't just someone which we read about in a book—he is the living Son of God who will return to the earth and will again demonstrate his power over the grave. Yet just as the two sisters had to learn, he is not just someone who is going to change things in that future day, but he can change things *today* (Psalm 46:1). This sign movingly demonstrates the power and the desire of the Lord Jesus Christ to work in the lives of his disciples at the present time and forever, not just in the last day. He is a very present help in time of trouble and he has the power to bring us from death to life. May a recognition of this cause us to trust in him and to fervently proclaim with Martha:

> "...Yea, Lord: I believe that thou art the Christ, the Son of God, which should come into the world." John 11:27

Christ in Bethabara

The story begins with the Lord Jesus Christ fleeing from the people. He had recently been at the temple during the feast of dedication (John 10:22) and he had sought to teach the Jews about his special relationship with the

Father. He and the Father were one. His thoughts were the Father's thoughts, his goals were the same as the Father's goals. He did what the Father taught him (John 5:19). Sadly, the Jews could not comprehend his sayings and subsequently sought to stone him for his "blasphemy":

> "The Jews answered him, saying, For a good work we stone thee not; but for blasphemy; and because that thou, being a man, makest thyself God." John 10:33

Instead of understanding the Lord's words to mean that he spoke the words of God and thought in the same way as God, they understood him to say that he literally was God—they completely misunderstood what Christ had said. As the dialogue progressed, things continued to get worse. The Lord's words were still misunderstood and the Jews tried once more to capture him:

> "Therefore they sought again to take him: but he escaped out of their hand." John 10:39

Jerusalem was becoming dangerous for the Lord Jesus. More and more, people were becoming violent toward him. Just a few chapters prior the Jews had tried to stone him (John 8:59). Now they had tried again, this time with more resolve! As a result of this violence and hatred against him, the Lord withdrew for a while into the wilderness.

> "And went away again beyond Jordan into the place where John at first baptized; and there he abode." John 10:40

The Resurrection of Lazarus

From Jerusalem, the Lord Jesus went northeast toward the Jordan river. Upon arriving at the river, he crossed over and went to where John had first been baptizing. From the reference in John 1:28, this appears to be Bethabara, a fairly isolated location somewhere on the other side of the Jordan. From there, he could preach undisturbed by the Jewish rulers and their treachery and he could preach to people who had a reverence for the word of God. This was where John had begun his preaching and where people remembered him. They remembered his words and his presence—and in Christ, they saw a fulfillment of his words.

> "And many resorted unto him, and said, John did no miracle: but all things that John spake of this man were true. And many believed in him there." John 10:41-42

As a contrast to the Jews of Jerusalem who desired to kill the Lord, the people in Bethabara and the surrounding area were receptive to the gospel. The Lord's ministry in this area was highly successful—and it was during this campaign that a family in Bethany was troubled by sickness. A man named Lazarus, dear to the Lord Jesus and to his disciples had become deathly ill.

The Family from Bethany

> "Now a certain man was sick, named Lazarus, of Bethany, the town of Mary and her sister Martha. (It was that Mary which anointed the Lord with ointment, and wiped his feet with her hair, whose brother Lazarus was sick.)" John 11:1-2

It was in Bethany that a mighty trial would come upon two faithful sisters and their brother. Not much is known about Lazarus before his death, in fact, his death is the first place where the Divine record introduces him (aside from the allusions in Luke 16:19-31). It's rare for a man to be known for his death, but such is the case with Lazarus—Scripture never records any of his words or any of his thoughts. However, despite the lack of detail about Lazarus' character, it can be said with surety that he was a deeply spiritual and committed brother. His name means "whom God helps," and it is the Greek version of Eleazar; to add to that, he was someone whom the Lord loved:

> "Therefore his sisters sent unto him, saying, Lord, behold, <u>he whom thou lovest is sick</u>." John 11:3

Lazarus was a man who was loved by the Son of God. Truly, he must have believed in Christ—aside from the disciples (John 13:1, John 21:20), Scripture only knows a few people whom Christ knew face to face and loved them. Lazarus was one of them. Two of the others were actually in his family:

> "Now Jesus <u>loved</u> Martha, and her sister, and Lazarus." John 11:5

This must have been a special family. Not only was Lazarus loved by Christ, but both of his sisters were as well. The only other person who fits into this category is the rich young ruler:

> "The Jesus beholding him <u>loved him</u>, and said unto him, One thing thou lackest: go thy way, sell whatsoever thou hast, and give to the poor, and thou

The Resurrection of Lazarus

shalt have treasure in heaven: and come, take up the cross, and follow me." Mark 10:21

Aside from the disciples, there were only four people with whom Christ came into contact and loved. This helps to show how special Lazarus was—he was a dearly loved friend of Christ. Before his death, he must have had some type of interaction with the Lord to create this friendship. It appears as though Christ often stopped by the house in Bethany, so perhaps that was how this relationship developed (Luke 10:38, John 12:1). Yet not only was he known by the Lord Jesus, he was also known and loved by Christ's disciples.

> "These things said he: and after that he saith unto them, <u>Our friend</u> Lazarus sleepeth; but I go, that I may awake him out of sleep." John 11:11

Lazarus was a friend of the Lord and a friend of his disciples. Though there is never a word recorded which he spoke, his mind must have been full of spiritual concepts—and sadly, this wonderful brother had become deathly ill. Something had taken hold of him and he could not seem to get better. Their family appears to be fairly wealthy, since they could afford a tomb (John 11:38) and later Mary anointed Christ with extremely expensive ointment (John 12:5). It seems likely, then, that these sisters would have hired the best physicians to treat their dying brother. Yet as the days passed, Lazarus only seemed to get sicker and sicker. Soon the life began to fade from his eyes—the sisters didn't want to trouble the Lord Jesus, they knew that it was extremely dangerous for him to come back near Jerusalem—where the Jews had tried to stone him—yet there was nothing else to do! Their brother was about to die.

The Message

Eventually Martha and Mary agreed that they would send a message to the Master. They wouldn't ask him to come—Martha had already learned the foolishness of demanding things of the Lord (Luke 10:40). Instead of demanding, they would simply state their need—Christ would know what they wanted and surely he would do right.

> "Therefore his sisters sent unto him, saying, Lord, behold, he whom thou lovest is sick." John 11:3

It was a simple message. Whatever it was that he chose to do they would trust and follow. They merely mentioned the problem, trusting in Christ's solution. It was a similar type request to what the Lord's mother had said earlier in the gospel:

> "And when they wanted wine, the mother of Jesus saith unto him, They have no wine." John 2:3

This is the type of statement which comes from someone who has a full and complete trust in the one to whom they are speaking. They know the problem and they have no idea how to solve it, but they know that the Lord has an answer—even if it is not the one which is expected. These two exceptional sisters were the same way, and we do well to learn from them. Sometimes the most heartfelt and sincere prayers are uttered when we simply lay the need before God—knowing and believing that He will do what is best.

Thus the sisters waited. It's probable that each day they came to their brother's bedside to see if he had miraculously improved—if perhaps the Lord had chosen to heal him from afar. Often they looked to the east for the messenger returning with a group of thirteen men. Yet each day their hopes were never realized.

Glorified

While the sisters tended to their feeble brother, the message reached the Master and his disciples. It was clear what the sisters wanted from Christ—they wanted healing for their brother. Yet the Lord knew that things had to be different. He knew that there was a greater purpose for this sickness. It wasn't just about Lazarus, but this sickness would be used for God's glory:

> "When Jesus heard that, he said, This sickness is not unto death, but for the glory of God, that the Son of God might be glorified thereby." John 11:4

This was the response of Christ to the messenger—thus, this was the message which the sisters received from the Lord. The messenger came back alone and Lazarus didn't miraculously recover. In fact, it appears as though that Lazarus had already died when the sisters received the message from the Lord! Bethabara was probably up in the north and within a day's journey of Galilee (cp. John 1:28-29, John 1:43; in one day Christ went from Bethabara to Galilee)—so it was fairly far away from Bethany, which was in the south. Most likely, the journey from Bethabara to Bethany was about a three or four day's journey. With this knowledge, an approximate time table can be worked out:

- Lazarus had been dead for four days by the time that Christ arrived in Bethany:

    "Then when Jesus came, he found that he had lain in the grave four days already." John 11:17

- Supposing that it took the Lord four days to journey to Bethany, Lazarus would have died on the day that Christ departed from Bethabara (notice that when the Lord left, Lazarus was already dead; John 11:14, thus, four days is the maximum amount of time that the journey could have taken).

- The Lord received the message two days before he left:

    "When he had heard therefore that he was sick, he above two days still in the same place where he was." John 11:6

If Lazarus died the day that Christ left Bethabara, then that means that when the Lord received the message, Lazarus still had two days to live. Again, assuming that it was a four day journey, the messenger would have arrived back with the sisters two days after their brother had died. The computation comes up the same if the distance is three days (notice that even if the distance was only *one day*, the point is still valid; Lazarus would have been dead by the time that the sisters received Christ's response). The messenger would have returned two days after the death of Lazarus. Lazarus was likely already sealed in the tomb when the messenger came to the sisters and relayed the words of the Lord:

The Resurrection of Lazarus

"This sickness is not unto death, but for the glory of God, that the Son of God might be glorified thereby."

How these words would have struck Mary and Martha—how could this sickness not be unto death?! By the time they received this message, their brother had been dead for two days already! What did this mean? How could the Lord have been wrong? They would have wrestled with his words.

Certainly they trusted him, but it just didn't make sense that he could say something like that. He was the one that they believed to be the Messiah (John 11:27), he was the Son of God. How could he make a mistake? One can simply picture the two sisters repeating these words over and over, trying to make sense of them. Yet there was even more to the story and more to the hurt of the sisters—the Lord received the message *before* Lazarus died. He *could* have healed him from Bethabara, just as he had done with the nobleman's son—but he didn't. Maybe he even could have rushed down to Bethany and saved Lazarus before he fell asleep (John 11:21). Yet he didn't. *Why* had the Master chosen to let their brother die? Why had he *not even come* with the messenger?

He had sent back a message, but his words seemed almost cold and detached from them—there was no empathy with their sorrow, no words of encouragement. To even make the matter even more confusing, the Lord had said that this sickness was for the *glory of God*. Again, how could this be if Lazarus wasn't even sick anymore?—he was dead!

The faith of these two sisters was being tried. There were perhaps days when they were angry with the Lord and felt completely deserted by him. Yet then there were days when they remembered his words and remembered who he was. Surely they would have struggled with what had just happened.

Yet in all things, the Lord Jesus Christ knew what he would do. When he said that this sickness was not unto death, this was truly what he meant. The Master was and is never wrong. As he would say later on the record, Lazarus was merely sleeping:

> "These things said he: and after that he saith unto them, Our friend Lazarus sleepeth; but I go, that I may awake him out of sleep." John 11:11

In the mind of Christ, Lazarus was only asleep, and he would wake soon. Certainly he had died, but his death was not to last, and therefore it was more akin to sleep than death. This is the same type of language which the Lord used when speaking of Jairus' daughter.

> "He said unto them, <u>Give place: for the maid is not dead, but sleepeth</u>. And they laughed him to scorn. But when the people were put forth, he went in, and took her by the hand, and the maid arose." Matthew 9:24-25

It was the same type of situation when Jairus' daughter had died. Christ did not see her death as an actual death—he was going to raise her. Thus, her death was merely sleep. Often the Lord operated with this type of thinking; many times when he spoke of death and life, he wasn't speaking of temporary death or temporary life, but that which is eternal. When he promised his followers that they would be saved from death, he never meant that they would not die—but that their death would only be sleep, because one day they would awake from that sleep.

> "Verily, verily, I say unto you, He that heareth my word, and believeth on him that sent me, hath everlasting life, and shall not come into condemnation; but if passed from death unto life." John 5:24

Those who follow Christ pass from death to life. They move from a state of eternal death to a state of eternal life. By the grace of God, that life will be granted to them when the Lord Jesus returns (Titus 1:2). Again, just a few chapters later, the Lord said the same thing:

> "Verily, verily, I say unto you, If a man keep my saying, he shall never see death." John 8:51

Those who followed Christ would never die—eternally. They would have the promise of eternal life and could fall asleep in the assurance that one day they would rise from the grave. This was the way that the Lord often spoke and the way that he often thought. His understanding of the resurrection and his faith in the power of the Father was so great that death for a believer was merely sleep. So it was with the death of Lazarus. He was only sleeping and would one day rise again—yet not only would he rise again at the last day (John 11:24), but the Lord would raise him even sooner.

In this, the glory of God would be shown. "This sickness is not unto death, but for the glory of God, that the Son of God might be glorified thereby." Lazarus would soon wake and because of his resurrection, God would be glorified. Through this miracle the mighty power of God over the grave was demonstrated, and many of the Jews came to believe in Christ (John 11:45)—God was glorified through it. Yet in an even greater sense, this miracle was for the glory of the Father (and the son) because it set in motion the process which brought the Lord Jesus to the cross—the time in which God's righteousness was proclaimed and Christ was raised up to glory. The Lord Jesus spoke of his death in this way:

> "And Jesus answered them saying, The hour is come, that the Son of man should be glorified." John 12:23

The Lord's time of death was the time in which he would be glorified. Yet not only would it bring him glory, but it would also bring glory to his Father.

> "Now is my soul troubled; and what shall I say? Father, save me from this hour: but for this cause came I unto this hour. Father, glorify thy name. Then came there a voice from heaven, saying, I have both glorified it, and will glorify it again." John 12:27-28

The Lord was troubled about his "hour," and in that distress, he prayed that God would glorify His name. God's response was that He had glorified His name in the past—and that His name would be glorified again, presumably through Christ's "hour," or his death. Thus, the death and resurrection of Christ was not only for the glory of the son but also for the glory of the Father. It brought honor to both—and it was the resurrection of Lazarus which assured the Lord's death at the hand of the Jews (John 11:53). Again, this same thing was said in the next chapter:

The Resurrection of Lazarus

> "Therefore, when he was gone out, Jesus said, Now is the Son of man glorified, and God is glorified in him." John 13:31

These words were said by the Lord once Judas departed from supper on his infamous mission. Christ knew what was about to take place, and he said that it was for the glory of the Father and the son. This was the meaning of Christ's message to the sisters. Lazarus' death was not an eternal death—he would soon be raised to life again. Yet through his resurrection, God would be glorified—his power would be shown and many would believe; but even more, this event would lead to the ultimate glorification of the Father and the son. The resurrection of Lazarus was what eventually brought the death of Christ.

Truly, the message from the Lord to the sisters was a message of hope. It was a message which proclaimed that Lazarus would soon live again, and it was a message which intimately connected the death of Lazarus to the Lord's own death—showing that he very much could empathize with the agony of the sisters. Unfortunately, with their brother dead and in the tomb, with their minds clouded by sadness, the underlying encouragement and depth of the message was probably lost upon Mary and Martha, and they would have received it with despondency and dejection.

Love for the Family

Yet this was not the intention. Though they may have been frustrated by the lack of the Lord's presence and the lack of a miracle, Christ's message towards them and his subsequent actions were all based upon his love for the family. John made sure to notify his readers of this—he wanted to be certain that the Lord's love was not ignored.

> "Now Jesus loved Martha, and her sister, and Lazarus." John 11:5

All of Christ's actions towards this family were based upon his love. He dearly loved this family, and they knew that he did, but it seems as though they may not have understood the extent to which the Lord loved them. When the sisters sent the message to Christ, they wrote "He whom thou lovest is sick." The detail here is unseen in the English, but in the Greek, the word translated "lovest" is "phileo." Often in Scripture, "phileo" is used to denote something for which someone has an affection or for which they deeply care. Here are some examples:

> "And when thou prayest, thou shalt not be as the hypocrites are: for they <u>love to pray</u> standing in the synagogues and in the corners of the streets, that they may be seen of men. Verily I say unto you, They have their reward." Matthew 6:5

The religious rulers of the day *loved* to pray for show. This type of prayer was something which brought them great pleasure and something in which they delighted. This is the sense of the word "phileo." Again, the Lord used the word in the same way later in the gospel of Matthew:

> "He that <u>loveth</u> father or mother more than me is not worthy of me: and he that <u>loveth</u> son or daughter more than me is not worthy of me." Matthew 10:37

The thrust of the Lord's message here was that his disciple could not delight in their parents, their children, or any of the rest of their family more than they delight in the Lord Jesus Christ! He should be the one who commands their greatest affection and who brings them their greatest joy. One last example of "phileo" helps to solidify the meaning:

> "He that <u>loveth</u> his life shall lose it; and he that hateth his life in this world shall keep it unto life eternal." John 12:25

Those who had a deep affection and care for their worldly life would find that eternal life had slipped from their grasp—the Lord was exhorting his followers to put aside their affection for the things of this life! Throughout Scripture, "phileo" love tends to describe a feeling of deep care and fondness.

In the case of Lazarus, the Lord Jesus had this special affection for him, and the sisters knew it. Yet there was an aspect of the relationship between Christ and Lazarus which the sisters may not have known. When John wrote "Now Jesus loved Martha, and her sister, and Lazarus..." the word for "loved" isn't "phileo." It's a different Greek word altogether. The word used there is "agapao," which is the root word for what is commonly called "agape" love.

This type of love is quite different than "phileo." In fact, it's entirely possible to have "agape" toward someone without ever feeling "phileo." "Agape" refers to a selfless love—it is a love which doesn't have to do with affection or feelings. Instead it is connected to actions and thoughts. Here are some of its uses:

> "Ye have heard that it hath been said, Thou shalt <u>love</u> thy neighbor, and hate thine enemy. But I say unto you, <u>Love</u> your enemies, bless them that curse you, do good to them that hate you, and pray for them which despitefully use you, and persecute you." Matthew 5:43-44

In speaking these words, the Lord Jesus helped to disassociate "agape" from feelings. Unlike "phileo," "agape" doesn't really relate to the way that someone feels toward something else—someone may be your enemy and you may not feel an affection with them, but Christ commanded us to love our enemies. We are to "do good" to them. This is the essence of "agape." It is a love which is selfless and willing to go *against* what one may feel at the moment.

> "<u>Charity</u> suffereth long, and is kind; <u>charity</u> envieth not; <u>charity</u> vaunteth not itself, is not puffed up, doth not behave itself unseemly, seeketh not her own, is not easily provoked, thinketh no evil." 1 Corinthians 13:4-5

Again, this list doesn't focus on feelings, rather it focuses on characteristics and actions—"seeketh not her own." This type of love is willing to sacrifice for someone else. It is willing to give up one's own desires for the good of another. In addition to "phileo," the Lord Jesus also had "agape" for Lazarus—the Lord loved Lazarus' character and was willing to sacrifice for him. While the sisters knew the affection that Christ had for their brother, they didn't seem to realize the selfless and sacrificing love which Christ had for him and for the two of them—they only used the word "phileo" in their note to the Master.

Yet John specifically pointed out Christ's "agape" for all three of them. Though the two sisters didn't realize Christ's love, John wanted his readers to know. In the next verse, the Lord would do something which may have seemed completely callous and unfeeling—yet John, guided by the spirit, wanted to make sure that his readers did not misinterpret Christ's actions.

> "Now Jesus loved Martha, and her sister, and Lazarus. When he had heard therefore that he was sick, he abode two days still in the same place where he was." John 11:5-6

After the Lord Jesus received the message about Lazarus, he waited in Bethabara for two days before leaving to Bethany—but he did this out of love! The actions of the Lord are not to be misunderstood—it was *because* of his love for the family that he stayed even longer. It's quite probable that he didn't want to stay there—he longed to go down and help! He didn't like to think of his friends in pain and sorrow. Yet he loved them and knew that this trial and this affliction would lead them closer to the Kingdom of God. That's why he stayed. The Lord Jesus Christ loved Martha, and her sister, and Lazarus.

Twelve Hours

The two days would have felt ever so long. The Lord, being full of compassion, knew that his friends were suffering. He wanted to go down to them, but he had to wait. Finally, the two days passed and the Lord Jesus was ready to go down to the family whom he loved.

> "Then after that saith he to his disciples, Let us go into Judaea again. His disciples say unto him, Master, the Jews of late sought to stone thee; and goest thou thither again?" John 11:7-8

The idea of going back to the place where they had almost died was not a popular idea with the disciples. They were happy out in Bethabara—it was safe and many people were responding to the gospel. The thought of going to raise Lazarus wouldn't have even passed through their mind. The last that they had heard about their friend, he was going to get better—"this sickness is not unto death." As far as they knew, Lazarus was on the mend—why would they go back into Judaea where people wanted to kill the Master?

In their minds, Judaea was not a safe place to go—for Christ or for them. As his disciples, if he were stoned, they would probably be stoned as well (John 11:16; John 18:8-9; notice that Jesus had to specially request safety for his disciples). The request of Christ was one which set them on edge. Yet Christ was ready with an answer.

> "Jesus answered, Are there not twelve hours in the day? If any man walk in the day, he stumbleth not, because he seeth the light of this world. But if a man walk in the night, he stumbleth, because there is no light in him." John 11:9-10

The words of the Lord would have been received by the disciples with confusion—perhaps frustration. How they would have longed to understand what he meant! Constantly he was speaking to them with symbols and allegories, and so often they misunderstood. They would have tried to make sense of what he meant by the twelve hours and the light and the darkness—but in the

The Resurrection of Lazarus

ensuing discourse none of the disciples said anything about these few sentences or even referred to them. They must have been utterly confounded! Yet these words were filled with depth and richness, and they contain the reason why the Lord Jesus was not afraid to go back into Judaea.

There were twelve hours in the Jewish day. It lasted from the time that the sun rose to the time when the sun set—approximately 6:00 AM to 6:00 PM. Thus, it was considered day during the time in which the sun illuminated the world. In symbol, the Lord was that sun (Malachi 4:2). He was the light of the world (John 8:12, John 9:5). As long as he was in the world, the world was filled with light and it was considered day time.

The Lord Jesus knew that his time in the world was not yet up. The Master was aware of how much time he had left. Eventually, that final hour would come upon him and the twelve hours would be over. On the last night of his life, Christ prayed to his Father:

> "These words spake Jesus and lifted up his eyes to heaven, and said, Father, <u>the hour is come</u>; glorify thy Son, that thy Son also may glorify thee." John 17:1

It was now the final hour of the Lord Jesus Christ's life. The twelve hours of the day had been spent. The light was going out. Yet all of the time before this was still the day. The light was still shining strong and it wasn't time for it to pass over the horizon.

Thus was the main point which Christ was presenting to the disciples—he was the light of the world and it was not yet his hour! There would still be light for a little while longer. He was not going to die before the time, as long as they walked with him—walked in the light—they would be safe. Only if they sought to walk contrary to Christ, or to walk in darkness, would they find themselves in danger. Once they departed from him they were no longer in the light and they would fall. "But if a man walk in the night, he stumbleth." It isn't a coincidence, then, that John later recorded that Judas went out into the "night" when he betrayed the Lord Jesus Christ.

> "He then having received the sop went immediately out: <u>and it was night.</u>" John 13:30

Judas had chosen to walk in darkness. He had chosen to depart from the light of the world, and because of that choice, he would stumble.

For the moment, all of the disciples had this same choice before them. They could walk in either the light or the darkness. They could walk with Christ or without him. If they walked in the light, they would be safe. It was not yet night (Luke 22:53). They could go down to Judaea and not worry about the danger, Yahweh would give His angels charge over them and they would be protected. After speaking these words, Christ then began to tell them about Lazarus.

Sleeping Lazarus

> "These things said he: and after that he saith unto them, Our friend Lazarus sleepeth; but I go, that I may awake him out of sleep." John 11:11

The Resurrection of Lazarus

They were to go into Judaea so that they might wake up Lazarus from sleep—yet again, this comment did not register with the disciples. Why did the Lord think it so imperative to wake Lazarus?

> "Then said his disciples, Lord, if he sleep, he shall do well. Howbeit Jesus spake of his death: but they thought that he had spoken of taking of rest in sleep." John 11:12-13

The disciples remembered what Christ had said to the messenger—"this sickness is not unto death," and they put that together with him sleeping. In their minds, this sleep was probably how he was going to heal! If he just continued to rest, he would slowly recuperate and come back to health. To the disciples, this was the ideal situation—why was the Lord so intent on going back to Judaea? Again, the Jews had just sought to stone him there. The disciples just didn't understand.

> "Then said Jesus unto them plainly, Lazarus is dead. And I am glad for your sakes that I was not there, to the intent ye may believe; nevertheless let us go unto him." John 11:14-15

Now the disciples could grasp a bit of his meaning. Lazarus was dead. Despite the fact that the sickness was not unto death, for some reason, Lazarus was no longer alive. Perhaps this was where things started to come together for the disciples. Christ had said that he was going to go back to Bethany so that he might "awake him out of sleep." If sleep was death, then Christ was planning on waking Lazarus out of death—he was planning on resurrecting him! Could it be that at this point the disciples started to understand? Possibly. Nevertheless, there was something at this point that filled Thomas with courage and caused him to proclaim his willingness to go back to Judea and die with the Master.

> "Then said Thomas, which is called Didymus, unto his fellowdisciples, Let us also go, that we may die with him." John 11:16

Though it doesn't appear as though Thomas understood the Master's words about traveling in the light and the safety that would come from it, his rallying call was courageous. It appears as though it inspired the rest of the disciples to follow their Lord from Bethabara to Bethany.

The Lord's Arrival

The scene in Bethany was quite troubling. When the Lord arrived at the city, Lazarus had already been dead for four days, and many of "the Jews" from Jerusalem had come to comfort the family.

> "Then when Jesus came, he found that he had lain in the grave four days already. Now Bethany was nigh unto Jerusalem, about fifteen furlongs off: and many of <u>the Jews</u> came to Martha and Mary, to comfort them concerning their brother." John 11:17-19

It was "the Jews" from Jerusalem who had originally sought to stone Christ when he escaped to Bethabara (John 10:31). Now, perhaps even the same Jews were present with the two sisters. Somehow their family had connections with the ritualistic Jews from Jerusalem and these people had come from Jerusalem to Bethany (about a two mile journey) to mourn with the family.

The Resurrection of Lazarus

The house would have been a place of great activity—as it was in Jairus' house when his daughter died. His house was filled with mourners and those who were playing instruments.

> "And when Jesus came into the ruler's house, and saw the minstrels and the people making a noise…"
> Matthew 9:23

When Jairus' daughter died, people came to his house to mourn with him and to play music. It probably would have been the same at the house in Bethany, maybe even more so considering that a whole group of people had come from Jerusalem. There would have been quite a bit of activity. Thus, as Christ came toward the city, he didn't actually enter (John 11:30). He stayed outside the city gates.

Instead of going into the city himself, perhaps he sent one of the disciples, or maybe more than one into the city to alert the sisters to the fact that he was there (John 11:20). Somehow Martha found out that the Master had come.

What emotion would swell up within this sister's heart as she heard that Jesus had come! The Lord had finally come to them. They had waited for him to come and they had wondered if he ever would—now, he was just outside of their city. He had not deserted them—yet he had left them for a few days, surrounded by their sorrow and without answers.

Their Lord had seemingly neglected their brother. Why? Martha and Mary could not understand. Christ was their *friend*. He *loved* Lazarus. Yet as their brother suffered and finally died, no healing came from the Lord. To add to that, he had actually told the sisters in his message that Lazarus' sickness would not be unto death—but it did! Their brother had been in the tomb for four days. For those last four days, their hearts were filled with grief and confusion. Why had this been allowed to happen when it could have been so easily stopped? Thoughts like this would have troubled Mary and Martha's minds as they mourned for their brother. Yet soon those thoughts would be calmed. The Lord Jesus Christ had come.

As soon as Martha heard that Jesus had come, she quietly and quickly slipped out of the house without drawing the attention of the Jews. Since these people had wanted to kill Christ before, they were still quite dangerous to him and she didn't want them to follow her outside of the city. This was a similar type of situation to that which had existed during the feast of tabernacles, when the Jews wanted to kill the Lord for healing on the Sabbath. Out of propriety, everything was to be done in secret.

> "But when his brethren were gone up, then went he also up unto the feast, not openly, <u>but as it were in secret</u>. Then the Jews sought him at the feast, and said, Where is he?" John 7:10-11

When the situation was dangerous, Christ tried to stay out of the public eye for a while until he needed to be exposed for the purpose of preaching (cp. John 7:14). So it was that his presence at this point was to be hidden for the time being. Martha sought to slip out of the house unnoticed. Thankfully, all of the Jews seemed to be occupied with comforting Mary (John 11:31, 45), so Martha was able to escape from the house without their notice.

The Resurrection of Lazarus

While Martha went to the Lord, Mary stayed behind in the house and one is left wondering why she did this. Mary seemed like she was the one who always wanted to be with Christ—if he was present, she was there, at his feet. Yet why was it that she did not go to see him at this point? Perhaps there are a few answers, but it seems as though two reasons may have come together and kept her away. First, she appears to have been stricken with grief much more than her sister. She was filled with sadness—when she finally saw Christ, she could not contain her weeping (John 11:32). This could be why the mourners were so focused upon her rather than Martha. Mary was smitten by her grief. Secondly, perhaps Mary had somehow come into contact with the dead body of her brother. If this was the case, she would have been unclean.

> "He that toucheth the dead body of any man shall be unclean seven days. He shall purify himself with it on the third day, and on the seventh day he shall be clean: but if he purify not himself the third day, then the seventh day he shall not be clean." Numbers 19:11-12

If anyone touched the body of a dead man, they would be unclean for seven days. On the third day of their uncleanness, they had to purify themselves with the water of separation. Four days after their purifying, they would be clean once again. Thus, if Mary had somehow touched Lazarus' body, she would have been unclean when the Lord arrived. Lazarus had been dead for four days, so she still had three more days until she was clean once again. It could be that one of these reasons is why Mary stayed in the house. Regardless, though she would have wanted to see the Master, she remained at the house. Martha went off to Christ.

Martha's Response

> "Then Martha, as soon as she heard that Jesus was coming, went and met him: but Mary sat still in the house. Then said Martha unto Jesus, Lord, if thou hadst been here, my brother had not died." John 11:20-21

As Martha came to the Lord, she had one thing in mind that she had to say to him. "If you would have been here, my brother would not have died." Constantly throughout those days the sisters had looked at each other through tear-stained eyes and said this (cp. John 11:32). Now, the thought remained in Martha's mind. All of her thoughts and all of her meditations upon Christ's message and upon her brother's death kept coming back to the questions which she could not dismiss—he could have prevented it—why didn't he? Why did he allow his friend to die? Yet she tempered her words with her belief in him. Though she didn't understand why he had done what he had done, she knew that the Lord still had the power of God.

> "But I know, that even now, whatsoever thou wilt ask of God, God will give it thee." John 11:22

Was there a hint here that Martha believed in Christ's power to raise Lazarus from the dead? Did she dare to believe that he might do such a thing? What else could she possibly mean? Of what other miracle could she be thinking? Martha knew that Christ had the power to bring life to the dead. He had done it two times before.

The Resurrection of Lazarus

Yet would it do it for them? Could he do it for someone upon whom corruption had already set in?

> "Jesus saith unto her, Thy brother shall rise again." John 11:23

This was the response—a purposefully vague answer to her plea, yet an answer which didn't entirely squash her hope. What did the Master mean when he said Lazarus would rise again? She couldn't allow herself to believe that Christ was referring to a present resurrection—she couldn't allow her hopes to rise to that level. Thus, she suggested a meaning to his words—waiting to see if he would disagree with her interpretation.

> "Martha saith unto him, I know that he shall rise again in the resurrection <u>at the last day</u>." John 11:24

Her answer to him demonstrated her understanding. While the Sadducees were arguing with the Pharisees about whether or not the resurrection existed (cp. Acts 23:7-8), Martha had learned from the Lord that it truly did (John 5:28-29). Make no mistake, this was an extremely spiritually minded family—Mary was one of the only people, even among the disciples, who realized that Christ would die and be buried (John 12:7). This was a special family which clung to the words of Christ and sought to understand them. Yet aside from showing her understanding, Martha's words also serve to show her desire for a concrete answer from the Lord. Would the Master correct her and tell her that this wasn't what he meant? Would he tell her that he meant that Lazarus would live again *that very day?* Imagine the suspense for this woman. Here she was, standing before the Son of God, holding on to her thread of hope, praying that Christ might give her brother life again.

> "Jesus said unto her, I am the resurrection, and the life: he that believeth in me, though he were dead, yet shall he live. And whosoever liveth and believeth in me shall never die. Believest thou this?" John 11:25-26

Before a miracle would be performed and before Martha's hopes would be realized, Martha had a lesson to learn. She had to realize that Christ was the resurrection and the life. He was the resurrection himself, no matter how long the person had been dead, no matter what year it was in the earth's history. He was the one who would perform the resurrection in the last day (John 5:28) and he could give life whenever he pleased. This was what Martha had to recognize.

She needed to realize the true power and the true status of the one who stood before her. She needed to understand the closeness of relationship between the Lord Jesus Christ and his Father. Earlier when she had come to the Lord and presented her plea, she admitted her belief that he could ask God for anything and God would give it to him (John 11:22). Yet her understanding was missing something. She didn't realize the extent of the relationship between Christ and his God. The Lord didn't *need* to *ask* God to raise Lazarus from the dead. He had the ability and he had God's power at his disposal! Christ had explained this previously:

> "For as the Father raiseth up the dead, and quickeneth them; even so the Son quickeneth whom he will." John 5:21

Just as God has the power to raise up anyone whom He desires at any time, so can the Lord Jesus Christ. He is

The Resurrection of Lazarus

the Son of God. The Father has given him the power. Martha had to realize this, and thus the Lord said to her, "I am the resurrection, and the life." Those who would believe him would never eternally die. If they died physically, they would be raised to life again. If they were alive when he returned, they would never die. Standing before her was a man who ruled over life and death. Did she believe this? She certainly did.

> "She saith unto him, Yea, Lord: I believe that thou art the Christ, the Son of God, which should come into the world." John 11:27

Uttered from the lips of Martha was a confession of faith which rivaled that of Peter (Matthew 16:16). She believed that he was the Messiah. Though she had been hurting for the past four days and though she was burdened with grief, she knew her Lord and she believed in his power. She knew that he had power over life and death. For Martha, her Lord was not just someone who would bring refuge and strength in the last day, but he was someone who would be a very *present* help in trouble. (Psalm 46:1). He could affect their lives at that moment, not just in the future—what a lesson for all believers to remember!

The Lord Jesus Christ should be someone that is a part of our everyday lives! We shouldn't just see him as someone who will come back to the earth and change things *in the future*. While this is an extremely important part of the work and role of the Lord Jesus, it isn't the only part of his role. We need to see Christ as a part of our lives *today*. We need to recognize that he, as the "resurrection and the life" is working to give us life each day.

> "Verily, verily, I say unto you, The hour is coming, and now is, when the dead shall hear the voice of the Son of God: and they that hear shall live. For as the Father hath life in himself; so hath he given to the Son to have life in himself...Marvel not at this: for the hour is coming, in the which all that are in the graves shall hear his voice, and shall come forth; they that have done good, unto the resurrection of life; and they that have done evil, unto the resurrection of damnation." John 5:25-26, 28-29

In this discourse, the Lord Jesus spoke of two resurrections—one which was occurring right at that instance, "The hour is coming, *and now is...*" and one which would occur in the future, "the hour is coming..." There was one resurrection which was occurring even as the Lord spoke those words—it was a spiritual resurrection, a passing from death to life of those who would believe and who would follow him—for those who would hear his voice. Those who were dead in their trespasses and sins could be given new life and trust in the promise of immortality. Christ would work in their lives at that very moment to take them from death to life. He does the same with us. He is a very present help in time of trouble. As it has been said, "I will never leave thee, nor forsake thee" (Hebrews 13:5). May we remember his presence at all times. Christ dwells with the faithful (John 14:23) and he will give them strength through trial (Philippians 4:13).

Mary's Response

Martha believed this and at that moment, she believed that he had the power to give life to her brother. Throughout this story, her belief fluctuated, but for the

The Resurrection of Lazarus

moment she remained strong. With this new conviction, Martha went back towards the house to tell her sister that the Master wanted to speak with her. Regardless of her possible uncleanness, he wanted to see her.

> "And when she had so said, she went her way, and called Mary her sister secretly, saying, The Master is come, and calleth for thee." John 11:28

Again, secrecy was of the upmost importance. Martha did not want the Jews to know that it was Jesus who had come to visit the sisters. She secretly called Mary to her and didn't even use Christ's name. Instead, she called him "the Master"—just in case someone happened to overhear them. The Master was there and wanted to see Mary. He called for her to come to him. As soon as she heard this, there was nothing holding her back. She rushed out of the house and outside the city, where Martha had met him.

> "As soon as she heard that, she arose quickly, and came unto him. Now Jesus was not yet come into the town, but was in that place where Martha met him." John 11:29-30

The Lord Jesus was outside of the city in the same place where Martha had come to him, probably to stay out of view of the Jews. These kind of emotional and private conversations did not need to be held in front of mockers. Unfortunately, despite Martha's efforts at secrecy, since many of the Jews were gathered around Mary to comfort her, when they saw her rush out of the house, they decided to follow her. Many of them guessed that she went towards the tomb so that she could weep there. Little did they know or expect who they were about to see and what was about to take place.

> "The Jews then which were with her in the house, and comforted her, when they saw Mary, that she rose up hastily and went out, followed her, saying, She goeth unto the grave to weep. Then when Mary was come where Jesus was, and saw him, she fell down at his feet, saying unto him, Lord, if thou hadst been here, my brother had not died." John 11:31-32

Mary saw the Lord Jesus and fell down at his feet. These were the feet which she would eventually anoint (John 12:3), and these were the feet at which she sat when she basked in his teaching (Luke 10:39). Now, she fell before them weeping. Again, she said the same thing to him as Martha—"Lord if thou hadst been here, my brother had not died." Mary was quite contemplative and would have constantly been trying to understand why this had happened and what Christ was teaching by it—yet her mind came up blank. All she could see was that her brother was dead—but he didn't need to be! This was a picture of pure grief. As the poor woman shuddered upon his feet, the Lord was moved.

> "When Jesus therefore saw her weeping, and the Jews also weeping which came with her, he groaned in the spirit, and was troubled." John 11:33

Mary bowed at his feet with tears flowing from her eyes. She was filled with sadness and yet conflict, seeking to hold on to her faith in the Lord. Yet at the same time, the Jews had followed her and were weeping as well—people whose characters were such that it is doubtful that they would have ever truly loved a brother like Lazarus. They were probably there as part of the ceremony, putting on a show and weeping fake tears.

The Resurrection of Lazarus

This hypocritical type of mourning was not uncharacteristic of the Jewish people. Zechariah addressed it in his prophecy.

> "When they had sent unto the house of God Sherezer and Regemmelech, and their men, to pray before the LORD, and to speak unto the priests which were in the house of the LORD of hosts, and to the prophets, saying, Should I weep in the fifth month, separating myself, as I have done these so many years?" Zechariah 7:2-3

Each year the Jews systematically wept and mourned, and they had just sent men to the temple to ask if they should continue to do this. They would do this every year in these specific months—this weeping was just an outward show! It was as though they could start crying on cue! This was not the type of worship which Yahweh desired, and He told them that:

> "Then came the word of the LORD of hosts unto me, saying, Speak unto all the people of the land, and to the priests, saying, When ye fasted and mourned in the fifth and seventh month, even those seventy years, did ye at all fast unto me, even to me? And when ye did eat, and when ye did drink, did not ye eat for yourselves, and drink for yourselves?" Zechariah 7:4-6

Their mourning had been completely focused on themselves and on making themselves appear "righteous"! This type of attitude had not disappeared during the Lord's day. In fact, he made reference to it.

> "Moreover when ye fast, be not, as the hypocrites, of a sad countenance: for they disfigure their faces, that

they may appear unto men to fast. Verily I say unto you, They have their reward." Matthew 6:16

The religious rulers of the day were full of this same type of hypocrisy. They would put on a show in order to appear like they were mourning. This seems to be the same type of thing that happened after Jairus' daughter died.

> "And he cometh to the house of the ruler of the synagogue, and seeth the tumult, and them that wept and wailed greatly. And when he was come in, he saith unto them, <u>Why make ye this ado, and weep?</u> the damsel is not dead, but sleepeth." Mark 5:38-39

When Jairus' daughter died, there were people all around the house making a big commotion and who were wailing loudly—this sounds fairly over-dramatic and exaggerated. Certainly people would be full of sorrow and weeping—but wailing loudly and making noise just doesn't seem quite appropriate. Christ confirmed this understanding when he said "Why make ye this ado…?" He referred to their mourning with a disparaging term—"ado," or an unnecessary fuss. Their weeping was unnecessary and overboard. Even though Christ was about to solve their situation and negate the need for mourning in the first place, he still stated that their way of mourning was an unnecessary extreme to begin with. This was the same type of thing which would have been seen with the Jews in Bethany. Their mourning was over-accentuated, fake, and full of hypocrisy—they never really loved Lazarus.

What a contrast this would have been to poor Mary. Her tears were real, they were from a sincere heart overflowing with sadness. The Jews were a complete

The Resurrection of Lazarus

opposite. Their hearts were full of deceit. They were there to put on an act. All throughout his ministry, the Lord hated this hypocrisy and denounced it.

> "Ye hypocrites, well did Esaias prophesy of you, saying, This people draweth nigh unto me with their mouth, and honoreth me with their lips; but their heart is far from me." Matthew 15:7-8

The Jews looked sincere on the outside, but their hearts were far removed from God. Their worship was hypocritical and Christ condemned it. Again, later in Matthew's gospel, similar words were recorded:

> "Who unto you, scribes and Pharisees, hypocrites! for ye make clean the outside of the cup and of the platter, but within they are full of extortion and excess." Matthew 23:25

This was the character of the Jews. They looked good on the outside but inside was sin. They were full of hypocrisy—and as Christ looked at their hypocritical weeping and Mary's sincere tears, he "groaned in the spirit, and was troubled." Rotherham's translation renders these words as follows:

> "Jesus, therefore, when he saw her weeping, and the Jews who came with her weeping, <u>was indignant in the spirit</u>, and troubled himself." John 11:33 Rotherham

This translation seems to fit the circumstances better. Constantly Christ was frustrated with the scribes and Pharisees, calling them "hypocrites!" or a "generation of vipers!" Their inconsistency caused him a great amount of indignation. So it was here. As he looked upon Mary and as he looked upon the Jews, the Lord Jesus Christ was filled with anger at their utter hypocrisy and insensitivity towards someone who was so truly full of grief. Yet soon he would change her grief to joy.

> "And said, Where have ye laid him? They said unto him, Lord, come and see. Jesus wept." John 11:34-35

Let it never be said that the Lord cannot feel the pain of his followers. He can. As the head of the body (Colossians 1:18), he knows the pain that exists in every one of its members. As he stood there outside the city, the emotion of the situation finally took hold of him. The utter anguish of Mary and her battle to believe in him, the long two days which he had to wait because of love for the sisters, the fact that Lazarus *had* to die for the glory of God, the reminder that this would have given him of his own death, and the complete stone-heartedness of the Jews all came together upon the man from Nazareth—and he wept. Truly, this man *can* be touched with the feelings of our infirmities. As he saw the sorrow of those whom he loved and thought about everything else going on around him, the Lord broke down—a truly touching picture of our Messiah. He isn't estranged from us, he isn't removed from our grief—but he weeps with those who weep. He cares for his sheep, and even though his actions and words towards us may not make sense to us at times—just as his message didn't for the sisters—the Lord Jesus knows ours trials and feels our pain. When we feel broken or when we feel shattered, let us not forget that. The Lord understands what we are going through.

> "Then said the Jews, Behold how he loved him!" John 11:36

The Resurrection of Lazarus

Yet the Jews did not understand. It wasn't for the dead that Christ wept. The Lord was not crying because of Lazarus—this would go against exactly what he had said at both of the other resurrections which he had performed! When the Lord Jesus raised up the widow of Nain's son, he specifically told her to "weep not"!

> "And when the Lord saw her, he had compassion on her, and said unto her, <u>Weep not</u>. And he came and touched the bier: and they that bare him stood still. And he said, Young man, I say unto thee, Arise." Luke 7:13-14

The widow was told to not weep! The same thing took place when the Master raised up Jairus' daughter.

> "And all wept, and bewailed her: but he said, <u>Weep not</u>; she is not dead, but sleepeth." Luke 8:52

In this verse, the Lord Jesus gave an explanation as to why the family of the dead was to "weep not." It was because those who had died were merely sleeping— they were about to be raised up to life again within just a few seconds! The same was true for Lazarus. Christ had just spent a conversation with the disciples seeking to teach them that Lazarus was only sleeping. Understanding that this was the case, it can be clearly seen that the Lord Jesus was *not* weeping because of his love for Lazarus. Just like the widow's son and just like Jairus' daughter, he would "weep not" because he knew that Lazarus would soon be awake again. Christ was weeping because he loved the sisters and he knew the pain that they felt. He wept because they were weeping. Yet the Jews did not understand this.

Even more, whereas some of the Jews simply did not understand, some of them even took the tears of Christ to be a sign of his weakness—they took it to be a sign of his helplessness in this situation. They callously sought to use this seeming picture of helplessness to disprove the Messiahship of the Lord:

> "And some of them said, Could not this man, which opened the eyes of the blind, have caused that even this man should not have died?" John 11:37

What a thing to say about the Son of God! If these mockers had known the power and authority of the one in whose presence they stood, they would have been flat on their faces before him. Yet they did not—and because of their ignorance they would perform even greater blasphemies (1 Corinthians 2:7-8). For the moment, they would suffice themselves by seeking to discredit Christ's miracles. They thought that through his tears he was showing that he was powerless in this situation—he was crying because Lazarus was dead and he could do nothing about it. Therefore they reasoned that if he could do nothing in this situation, perhaps he had actually done nothing in some of his other miracles—notably the man born blind. Perhaps their thoughts were as follows: "If this man was able to perform such a mighty miracle in giving sight to a man born blind, then could he not have prevented Lazarus from dying? Yet since he is weeping here, and since he appears to be powerless to change the situation, perhaps he actually couldn't have prevented Lazarus from dying. Therefore, if he couldn't have prevented the death of his friend, maybe he never actually brought sight to the blind!"

The Resurrection of Lazarus

The Jews were reverting right back to their tactics when they tried to call in the parents of the blind man! There they had sought to prove that he had never been blind in the first place. Now they were doing the same thing—seeking to prove that no miracle had really ever happened. Yet what was about to take place before them would be a miracle for which there would be no way around. Even those arrogant Jews would have to admit that this man had the power of God at his disposal.

> "Then gathered the chief priests and the Pharisees a council, and said, What do we? <u>for this man doeth many miracles?</u>" John 11:47

The resurrection of Lazarus would be a sign which would force the Jews to admit to the miraculous power of Christ (though they would still shut their eyes to its significance)—but for the time being, they would seek to discredit them and to mock the one whom God had sent. In fact, this mocking was just the predecessor for very similar ideas which the Lord would hear from the same people, very soon after this resurrection:

> "He saved others; himself he cannot save. If he be the King of Israel, let him now come down from the cross, and we will believe him. He trusted in God; let him deliver him now, if he will have him: for he said, I am the Son of God." Matthew 27:42-43

Similar words of blasphemy from the same ignorant group. Again they would seek to discredit the Lord and bring down the miraculous deeds which he did. "If he truly did all of these miracles, why can he not save himself?" The spirit of the words which the Lord heard on the cross were the same as the spirit of the words which were uttered just before the resurrection of

Lazarus. The Lord Jesus knew that he would hear these words on the cross— it had been prophesied long before (Psalm 22:8). Hearing these same type of words come from the same people would have deeply affected the Master. Here were men whose hearts were so hard that they would never turn. Through that hardness of their hearts, they would lead their nation to complete ruin (Matthew 23:37-39). The Lord was again filled with indignation for them and their remarks.

> "Jesus therefore again groaning in himself cometh to the grave. It was a cave, and a stone lay upon it." John 11:38

The Lord Jesus again felt the righteous anger rise up within him. These men had ridiculed the power of God—they had blasphemed the Holy Spirit. How this would have upset him! Yet he had not come for the purpose of dealing with the Jews. He now stood before the grave of Lazarus—and to add to all of the pressure and emotion which the Lord felt at that moment, Lazarus was buried in a tomb—just like what the Lord Jesus would be buried in. From the prophecy of Isaiah, Christ would have known that he was going to be buried in a tomb:

> "And he made his grave with the wicked, <u>and with the rich in his death</u>; because he had done no violence, neither was any deceit in his mouth." Isaiah 53:9

The Master most definitely would have known this passage. He would have known that he was to be buried with the rich, or in a tomb—and as he looked at the tomb before him, thoughts of his death would have been inevitable! The Jews were mocking, just like they would when he hung on the cross. He was looking at a tomb, which was similar to the tomb in which he would be buried. Bethany was nigh to Jerusalem (John 11:18). The anticipation and stress of the approaching day would have been unbelievable! Yet again, the Lord continued with the work which he had from his Father.

Resurrection

> "Jesus said, Take ye away the stone. Martha, the sister of him that was dead, saith unto him, Lord, by this time he stinketh: for he hath been dead four days." John 11:39

Something unimaginable was about to take place. The Lord Jesus commanded that the stone be removed from the tomb. The Jews would have looked at each other in horror—Lazarus had been dead for four days! Even Martha didn't know what to do with Christ's command! How could he want to do such a thing? The smell would be terrible and the situation was already delicate enough—they did not need to see their brother's dead body again.

Martha had learned earlier not to rebuke Christ (Luke 10:41-42). She was to follow him and trust him. Yet this time she didn't know what to do with his request. She couldn't hold it in—"Lord, by this time he stinketh: for he hath been dead four days!" Earlier when the Master had spoken to Martha, she had demonstrated an extraordinary faith. She had shown her belief that Christ could raise Lazarus and she had demonstrated her hope that he would do it that very day! What had happened?

Glimpses of the Master

The apostle John gave a little clue when he wrote the narrative—"Martha, the sister of him *that was dead*..." Clearly Martha was Lazarus' sister. John had already explicitly alerted his readers to this (John 11:1-2, 21). Why did he now see it as important to tell them this again, near the end of the record? The answer and the significance lies in the detail. John did *not* simply reaffirm that Martha was Lazarus' sister. He said that she was the sister of *him that was dead*. That's a key phrase. At this point, Martha's mind had slipped back into a temporal way of thinking, rather than an eternal. To her, Lazarus wasn't *sleeping*—he was *dead*. Thus, Martha spoke based off of this way of thinking. Her mighty faith which had been expressed just a few verses prior had slightly slipped. Let it be recognized and admitted that even the strongest faith can falter at times. This happened to Martha, yet in mercy, the Lord Jesus Christ lifted her up again:

> "Jesus saith unto her, Said I not unto thee, that, if thou wouldest believe, thou shouldest see the glory of God?" John 11:40

The Master had to remind his disciple that she had to *believe*. This is what he had told her before. If she would believe she would see the glory of God—this was an allusion back to Christ's first message, the message which had confused and possibly frustrated the sisters (John 11:4). The sickness was not unto death, but for the glory of God. Soon Martha would have the message worked out before her eyes. Soon she would see how her brother's sickness could bring glory to the Father. She just needed to believe.

> "Then they took away the stone from the place where the dead was laid. And Jesus lifted up his eyes,

and said, Father, I thank thee that thou hast heard me. And I knew that thou hearest me always: but because of the people which stand by I said it, that they may believe that thou hast sent me." John 11:41-42

After the encouragement from the Lord, Martha's protest ceased. She would trust. She would believe in his power. The stone was rolled away. It would have taken a number of men to do this—perhaps even the disciples helped. The men would have rolled the stone from the mouth of the cave and then quickly ran from the area before they could smell the body.

Once the stone had been removed, the Lord Jesus Christ thanked God for a miracle which hadn't yet been seen—so great was his faith. Amazingly, so much hung upon this miracle, yet the Lord unwaveringly believed in the power of His Father. Just think about what could have happened if Lazarus had not come forth from the tomb. The belief of the two sisters would have been completely crushed and their doubts would have been confirmed. The Jews could have taken Christ as a false prophet. Lazarus would have remained dead. So much relied upon this miracle being performed—and the faith of Christ never faltered. He knew the power of his Father, he knew that the resurrection of Lazarus was part of God's plan, and he trusted that God would perform the miracle—so much so that he thanked God for the performance of it before anyone could see that it had happened! Truly he is the *author* and *finisher* of faith.

The prayer was uttered and the Lord thanked his Father for hearing him—meaning that he had probably prayed for this resurrection sometime before this present prayer. Perhaps this was how the Lord knew that Lazarus was dead, back while he was in Bethabara (John 11:14). The Master was constantly in prayer—how many unrecorded prayers to the Father must have been uttered by the Lord Jesus!

This prayer, the one recorded just before Christ called to Lazarus, was a public prayer uttered for the sake of the multitude. It was a prayer which confirmed that the Lord had been praying for Lazarus to be given life again, and a prayer which showed that the power given to him had come from God. It was Yahweh's power given to His son in order that the Father might be glorified. Because it was God's power, this prayer and this miracle confirmed Christ as the one sent from God—"And I knew that thou hearest me always: but because of the people which stand by I said it, that they may believe that thou hast sent me." The prayer was for the faith of the people standing by. After the prayer, the Lord turned his attention to the tomb.

> "And when he thus had spoken, he cried with a loud voice, Lazarus, come forth." John 11:43

With a loud voice the Lord Jesus called out to his friend. He summoned the one who had been dead for four days. Imagine the silence from the crowd as everyone intently gazed at the cave. What would happen? Would the young man truly arise? Did this man from Nazareth actually have power to restore someone from the corruption of death? The air would have been tense. Yet suddenly, it could be seen that someone was coming out of the tomb!

> "And he that was dead came forth, bound hand and foot with grave clothes: and his face was bound

The Resurrection of Lazarus

about with a napkin. Jesus saith unto them, Loose him, and let him go." John 11:44

Immediately life surged back into his body and the corruption melted away. His flesh was restored and he began to walk out of the tomb. The faces of the Jews would have been painted with disbelief. They had thought that the tears of the Lord had been because he was helpless—yet now they saw Lazarus walking towards them! The one who had been dead for four days was now alive again! How could it be? How could someone possibly have the ability to do these things?!

How the sisters—especially Mary—would have ran to meet their brother! How they would have embraced him! Their brother was alive again! Earlier in the day, Martha had not dared to hold onto the hope that she might see him again before the last day. Yet now there he was. He was standing before them. It was an astonishing miracle—but at the same time, it was also an astonishing contrast with another resurrection which was soon to take place. Whereas there were many similarities between the resurrection of Lazarus and the resurrection of Christ, there were also a few contrasts—one of the major ones being that when the Lord Jesus came forth from the tomb, he was no longer bound with the grave clothes:

> "Then cometh Simon Peter following him, and went into the sepulchre, and seeth the linen clothes lie, and the napkin, that was about his head, not lying with the linen clothes, but wrapped together in a place by itself." John 20:6-7

Once the Lord Jesus was resurrected and once he departed from the tomb, he was no longer in his grave clothes. Those stayed behind in the tomb. It was not so with Lazarus. Instead, he "came forth, bound hand and foot with graveclothes." This is hugely symbolic! When the Lord Jesus Christ was raised up, he was raised up to life! He was raised to immortality! Lazarus was not. Though he was given new life again, there was a time when he eventually died once more. Lazarus was raised to mortality—he was still "bound" by sin and death. This was completely the opposite with the Master. When he was resurrected he was no longer bound by the grave. He had conquered it!

This also seems to be the reason for the different number of days which Christ and Lazarus spent in the grave. Lazarus was in the grave for four days—Martha stated that corruption had already set in. Yet it was completely different for the Lord Jesus Christ! He was only in the grave for three days (Matthew 12:40), and during those three days, no part of him saw corruption!

> "For David speaketh concerning him, I foresaw the Lord always before my face, for he is on my right hand, that I should not be moved: therefore did my heart rejoice, and my tongue was glad; moreover also my flesh shall rest in hope: because thou wilt not leave my soul in hell, <u>neither wilt thou suffer thine Holy One to see corruption</u>." Acts 2:25-27

Though Lazarus was four days in the grave and though his body saw corruption, the Lord Jesus was completely different. He was only in the grave for three days and he did not see corruption. This contrast serves to illustrate the same point as the prior contrast—everything about the resurrection of Lazarus shows that it was simply a resurrection to mortality! Certainly it was an amazing miracle, yet the contrasts between the resurrection of

Christ and the resurrection of Lazarus shows that one was raised up to mortality and one was raised up to immortality.

But there was one final contrast between the two resurrections, and again, this contrast emphasized the same thing as the others. The stone which closed off the Lord's tomb was rolled away by angels, God's immortal messengers—not by men.

> "And, behold, there was a great earthquake: for the angel of the Lord descended from heaven, and came and rolled back the stone from the door, and sat upon it." Matthew 28:2

While Christ had his tomb opened by one with immortality, Lazarus was the opposite. His tomb was opened up by men. Christ was brought into the world by an immortal and Lazarus was brought into the world by mortals. Again, this demonstrates one of the major differences between Christ's resurrection and Lazarus' resurrection—one was to immorality and one was to mortality. All of the little details which the apostle John recorded come together to show his readers that though Lazarus' resurrection was a picture of the future resurrection of Christ, it merely pointed forward to it. It was by no means as glorious. This is not at all to downplay the significance of the resurrection of Lazarus—rather, it is to magnify the resurrection of Christ! Even a miracle as significant and as breathtaking as the resurrection of a man dead for four days cannot fully show the glory of the resurrection of the Lord Jesus Christ.

Nevertheless, though this miracle paled in comparison with the greater resurrection to come, it was still an event which bridged the gap of what many saw between possible and impossible. It was a miracle which realized the faith of Martha, confirmed the faith of Mary, and even began new faith in some of the Jews. Those whose hearts had not been entirely hardened by their rituals and traditions actually began to believe in the Lord.

> "Then many of the Jews which came to Mary, and had seen the things which Jesus did, believed on him." John 11:45

For a number of the Jews who had come to comfort Mary, this sign was enough to begin their faith in Christ. Their hard hearts were softened and they believed. Yet for others, they refused to acknowledge his divine mission and origin. They would not believe, though one rose from the dead. These Jews took what they had seen and ran to the Pharisees—looking for some kind of explanation for what had just happened. Truly, the words of the Lord in the parable of the rich man and Lazarus had begun to be fulfilled:

> "And he said, Nay, father Abraham: but if one went unto them from the dead, they will repent. And he said unto him, If they hear not Moses and the prophets, <u>neither will they be persuaded, though one rose from the dead</u>." Luke 16:30-31

The rich man had pleaded that Lazarus be resurrected and sent to his brethren—if this could happen, he said, then his brethren would repent. Yet Abraham turned away his plea, saying that if they did not hear Moses and the prophets, then they would not truly turn though one rose from the dead. So it was—exactly the way that the Lord Jesus had said that it would be. A man named Lazarus (the name in the parable was not an accident!)

The Resurrection of Lazarus

had been raised from the dead, and some of the Jews still refused to believe. This unbelief would still hold true even after the Lord Jesus himself had risen (Matthew 28:11-13). This sign, the resurrection of Lazarus, impacted many of the Jews and they turned to Christ—yet there were some whose hearts were harder than stone and they refused to follow the Lord. This latter class found their way to the Pharisees to tell them what they had seen.

Gathering Together

> "But some of them went their ways to the Pharisees, and told them what things Jesus had done. Then gathered the chief priests and the Pharisees a council, and said, What do we? for this man doeth many miracles." John 11:46-47

Upon hearing what had been done, the religious rulers gathered together a council to determine what they should do about the Lord. They were in confusion—what should be done? Some newer translations help to make their question a bit more apparent. The rulers didn't have any idea what they should do!

> "So the chief priests and the Pharisees gathered the Council and said, 'What are we to do? For this man performs many signs.'" John 11:47 ESV

> "The chief priests, therefore, and the Pharisees, gathered together a sanhedrim, and said, 'What may we do? because this man doth many signs?'" John 11:47 YLT

Glimpses of the Master

What should they do? Christ was performing many signs—what should they say about that? Should they admit that he was a teacher sent from God or should they continue their opposition against him? It's almost as though this verse is showing another division amongst the rulers of Israel. They didn't know what to do. This miracle and this council only accentuated the division which had been brought about at the healing of the blind man.

> "Therefore said some of the Pharisees, This man is not of God, because he keepeth not the sabbath day. Others said, How can a man that is a sinner do such miracles? and there was a division among them." John 9:16

This division had really begun when the blind man had been healed, centering around the debate of whether or not the Lord Jesus was a sinner. He stood against the typical understanding of the law of Moses, yet he performed such astounding miracles! No one had ever brought sight to a man who had been born blind, and no one had raised up a man who had been in the grave for four days. How could he perform these things unless he was sent from God? It appears as though this same type of argument took place again amidst this council of the Jews. As John later testified, some of the rulers believed on Christ and some of them didn't—this clearly would have been a divided group:

> "Nevertheless among the chief rulers also many believed on him; but because of the Pharisees they did not confess him, lest they should be put out of the synagogue." John 12:42

The Resurrection of Lazarus

There were chief rulers who believed on the Lord Jesus. Thus, as this group came together to discuss, they could not come to a conclusion as to what to do about Christ! The only thing that both sides had in common was the acknowledgment that the Lord Jesus had actually performed miracles.

Amazingly, they were no longer trying to deny the miracles—the rulers finally realized that they couldn't be denied. Instead, both groups acknowledged his power. All throughout his ministry, his opposition had sought for signs, and now they had to admit that he had performed them. For the one group, these signs showed that he was a teacher sent from God.

> "There was a man of the Pharisees, named Nicodemus, a ruler of the Jews: the same came to Jesus by night, and said unto him, Rabbi, <u>we know that thou art a teacher come from God: for no man can do these miracles that thou doest, except God be with him.</u>" John 3:1-2

For Nicodemus and the others in the council who believed on Christ, the miracles were proof that he had come from God. Yet for the other side, the miracles seemed to have no effect. They were able to admit that they had taken place, but their eyes were closed to the significance!

It would seem quite odd that this acknowledgement of his power could come from the men who opposed him. How could they justify their opposition if they could admitted his miracles? How could they possibly agree together that Christ had performed many miracles and subsequently choose to kill him? Perhaps the answer is to be found within the law. In the book of

Deuteronomy, one of the laws implied that there was the possibility that a false prophet could perform miracles:

> "If there arise among you a prophet, or a dreamer of dreams, and giveth thee a sign or a wonder, and the sign or the wonder come to pass, whereof he spake unto thee, saying, Let us go after other gods, which thou hast not known, and let us serve them; thou shalt not hearken unto the words of that prophet, or that dreamer of dreams: for the LORD your God proveth you, to know whether ye love the LORD your God with all your heart and with all your soul." Deuteronomy 13:1-3

Perhaps it was that the Pharisees and the chief priests leaned upon this passage to support their unbelief in the Lord. Though he had performed all of these miracles, his teaching was contrary to the law (in their minds). As a result, they rejected him and chose to do as the law said.

> "And that prophet, or that dreamer of dreams, shall be put to death; because he hath spoken to turn you away from the LORD your God, which brought you out of the land of Egypt, and redeemed you out of the house of bondage, to thrust thee out of the way which the LORD thy God commanded thee to walk in. So shalt thou put the evil away from the midst of thee." Deuteronomy 13:5

According to the passage, the prophet was supposed to die. Ironically, they were the false prophets, not the Lord Jesus. They were the ones who should have been killed. Unfortunately, many people in the nation did not see it. Thus, there was one group which agreed with the Lord and there was another which believed he needed to die for his false ideas—soon, one of the latter group would stand forth and lead the council to its most despicable decision. Yet for the time being, the two groups were in confusion. What were they to do?

Nevertheless, despite their confusion, they knew that if things didn't change soon, they would be in trouble with the Romans. For these men, though some of them believed in the Lord Jesus, their belief did not outweigh their love for power. As John later wrote, they loved loved the praise of men more than the praise of God (John 12:42-43). They wanted to do anything that they could to prevent the loss of their power over the people.

Our Place and Our Nation

> "If we let him thus alone, all men will believe on him: and the Romans shall come and take away both our place and nation." John 11:48

Unhindered, the teaching and power of the Lord Jesus Christ would cause everyone to believe on him. This was something which all of the Pharisees and all of the chief priests opposed—they were afraid that if all the people began to believe on him, the people would lift him up as their king. This idea was not unfounded (John 6:15). Making Jesus their king would incite a major rebellion against Rome—and this was exactly what the rulers of Israel wanted to avoid. They wanted to keep the Romans appeased. This was why they later told Pilate that they had no king but Caesar:

"And it was the preparation of the passover, and about the sixth hour: and he saith unto the Jews, Behold your King! But they cried out, Away with him, away with him, crucify him. Pilate saith unto them, Shall I crucify your King? The chief priests answered, We have no king but Caesar." John 19:14-15

The chief priests did not want another king! They wanted to do whatever was necessary in order to keep the Romans at bay. If the Romans looked upon them favorably, then these men would be able to stay in power. However, as they stated at their council meeting, they feared that if Rome did not favor them, they would soon be out of power and out of a position—"the Romans shall come and take away both our place and nation." They would lose their status in the nation and they would even lose the nation itself.

If all of the people began to follow the Lord Jesus Christ, and if all of the people made him their king, then a rebellion against Rome would surely occur. This meant that the Romans would come to Judaea, crush the rebellion, and remove the religious leaders from power. This was not something which they wanted at all. The Jewish rulers loved their temple and they loved their power over the people. While some of the leaders believed in Jesus, they did not believe enough to lose their position of rulership for him. They wanted to do everything they could to prevent the Romans from coming. These were the thoughts and words of mere politicians! Never did they consult God, never did they even mention Him in all of their conversation. These men were ambitious politicians, and many of them were nothing else. They wanted to keep the Romans out and they would do whatever they could to do so. The irony

The Resurrection of Lazarus

of this is that *because* of the decision which was made there at the council—namely, the decision to kill the Lord Jesus Christ—the Romans came. Throughout his ministry, the Master warned the people of this. It wasn't his acceptance by the people that would bring the Romans—it was the rejection. In the parable of the vineyard, the Lord Jesus warned that the wicked husbandmen would be destroyed because they killed the messengers and because they killed the son.

> "But when the husbandmen saw the son, they said among themselves, This is the heir: come, let us kill him, and let us seize on his inheritance. And they caught him, and cast him out of the vineyard, and slew him. When the lord therefore of the vineyard cometh, what will he do unto those husbandmen? They say unto him, He will miserably destroy those wicked men, and will let out his vineyard unto other husbandmen, which shall render him the fruits in their seasons." Matthew 21:38-41

Because of their unfaithful stewardship and their murderous actions, the husbandmen would be destroyed—this is exactly as it came to pass! The husbandmen, or the religious rulers of Christ's day, were not destroyed by the Romans because all of the people began to follow their Savior—instead they were actually destroyed because of their rejection of the Son! Again, this same message was given to the scribes and Pharisees:

> "Wherefore, behold, I send unto you prophets, and wise men, and scribes: and some of them ye shall kill and crucify; and some of them shall ye scourge in your synagogues, and persecute them from city to city: that upon you may come all the righteous blood

shed upon the earth, from the blood of righteous
Abel unto the blood of Zacharias son of Barachias,
whom ye slew between the temple and the altar.
Verily I say unto you, All these things shall come
upon this generation." Matthew 23:34-36

All of those sent to them had been killed. That
generation rejected the prophets and even more,
rejected the Son. As a result of that, the blood of all of
the prophets would come upon them—the Romans
would rush upon their nation and leave a trail of
destruction in their path. Counter to the understanding
of the religious rulers, the desolation of Israel from the
Romans would not take place because of the people
supporting the Lord Jesus, it would happen because of
what the rulers were about to decide at that moment—
because of the ruling of one man. As that confusion
ensued amongst the council, that one man spoke above
the rest. This man was the high priest, and one of those
who didn't regard Christ's miracles; as he spoke up to
the council, his intentions became quite plain.

Caiaphas

"And one of them, named Caiaphas, being the high
priest that same year, said unto them, Ye know
nothing at all. Nor consider that it is expedient for
us, that one man should die for the people, and that
the whole nation perish not." John 11:49

Caiaphas was ruthless. As he raised his voice among the
council members, he said to them—"ye know nothing
at all." It was as though he looked at all of the
confusion and all of the deliberating and condemned
their lack of understanding. The confusion wasn't

needed. This man from Nazareth had clearly been causing problems—therefore as high priest, he used his authority to make a quick judgment. Clearly they could see that if this preaching continued, the Romans would come. If the Romans came, they would lose their position and the nation would be destroyed. Thus, the preaching must be stopped in order to save the nation—one man needed to die for the people, that the whole nation perish not. Jesus needed to die. This was the point at which the religious leaders became fully determined to destroy the Lord Jesus Christ—the one who was the resurrection and the life. They had sought to kill him before, but now there was a resolve in their decision which hadn't existed before. They must kill Jesus before he caused a major rebellion.

Based off of the way that Caiaphas denounced all of the other rulers, the rest of his words must have been said with a certain smugness—he thought that he was so wise! If they just put the man to death, there would be no more issue! It was expedient for them that this preacher died. Yet unknown to him, his plan would actually have the exact opposite effect than what he desired. As mentioned earlier, it would be the death of Christ which would seal Jerusalem's fate—because of his rejection by the Jewish people, the Romans would come and destroy the city. Yet there was more to Caiaphas' absolute lack of understanding than just the coming of the Romans. Caiaphas had stated that his plan was "expedient" for the Jews, yet it truly wasn't. Instead, completely counter to what Caiaphas understood, his plan was actually expedient for the Lord Jesus and his disciples. The death and resurrection of God's son had been planned from the very beginning:

> "But because I have said these things unto you, sorrow hath filled your heart. Nevertheless I tell you the truth; <u>It is expedient for you that I go away</u>: for if I go not away, the Comforter will not come unto you; but if I depart, I will send him unto you." John 16:6-7

The death, resurrection, and ascension of Christ to heaven were all part of the plan of God! Not only was it part of God's plan, but it was what needed to happen—it was "expedient" for the disciples. While Caiaphas smugly thought that he was full of wisdom, his proclamation was total nonsense. His idea of killing Christ wasn't at all expedient to the Jews—they killed their Messiah! As a result of this betrayal, their entire nation—including their beloved temple—was decimated by the Romans. The exact outcome that they were seeking to avoid, actually came upon them. Not only so, this decision wasn't only catastrophic for the Jews, but it was good for the Lord Jesus and his disciples! It was expedient for the believers! In this same account of the council, the apostle John actually went on to explain more about this decision's benefit for the followers of Christ.

> "And this spake he not of himself: but being high priest that year, he prophesied that Jesus should die for that nation; and not for that nation only, but that also he should gather together in one the children of God that were scattered abroad." John 11:51-52

Caiaphas' words, completely contrary to what he understood, were actually a prophecy. Being high priest that year, Yahweh worked through him and caused him to prophesy. Even though it might seem a bit strange that God would speak through a sinful and wicked man, this was not all together unheard of. There are a few other places where this took place—namely the prophecies of Balaam. Caiaphas, the ruthless and wicked high priest, had just made a prophecy through his words. In saying that one man should die for the people, Caiaphas meant that Jesus should die for all of the Jews. Yet John expanded this view of "the people." In the prophecy, "the people" didn't mean just the Jews—it meant all of the believers, all of the people of God, including the Gentiles! This was why John wrote, "and not for that nation only, but that also he should gather together in one the children of God…" The Lord Jesus would die, "not for that nation only" but for all of the children of God! In this way, the death of Christ would bring together all of the children of God into one (John 17:20-21)—into a unified body, "that the whole nation perish not." Christ's death would bring the Jews and the Gentiles together and would prevent them from perishing, from everlasting death! This prophecy was completely counter to what Caiaphas had meant. He had wanted the Lord Jesus to die for the sake of the nation of Israel, yet this was not at all what his words actually meant. Yet there was still a bit more irony to the words of Caiaphas—truly, God resists the proud and confounds their words.

Throughout this account of the Jewish council, John twice reminded his readers that Caiaphas was the high priest that year. This doesn't seem to be necessary—why not just mention it once?

> "And one of them, named Caiaphas, being <u>the high priest that same year</u>, said unto them, Ye know nothing at all." John 11:49

Again, he wrote the same thing just two verses later.

> "And this spake he not of himself: <u>but being high priest that year</u>, he prophesied that Jesus should die for that nation." John 11:51

In just a short space of three verses, John told his readers *twice* that Caiaphas was the high priest that year. Why? He could have just mentioned it at the beginning of the section and then not said it again. There must be some reason that it was written a second time in verse 51. Perhaps this was the reason—the Spirit wanted to draw attention to the fact that he was prophesying *as high priest*. During the Jewish year, there was a specific time in which the high priest was involved in prophecy—it was on the day of atonement and was part of the process of choosing which goat would be killed for the sacrifice:

> "And he shall take the two goats, and present them before the LORD at the door of the tabernacle of the congregation. And Aaron shall cast lots upon the two goats; one lot for the LORD, and the other lot for the scapegoat." Leviticus 16:7-8

Each year, on the day of atonement, the high priest was involved in prophesy. He would cast lots upon the two goats, determining which goat would be used for the sin offering for the people and which goat would be the scapegoat. Amazingly, this was exactly what Caiaphas, led by the Spirit to prophesy, had done! He had just unconsciously made a prophecy about the sin offering! Through his words, he chose the Lord Jesus as that offering. Little did he know that he was doing this. Yet this is perhaps what John was seeking to show. *Being high priest*, Caiaphas prophesied that Christ would die, not for that nation only, but for all of the people of God.

The Resurrection of Lazarus

Caiaphas chose the Lord Jesus for the sin offering—he fulfilled the type of the casting of the lot and the two goats on the day of atonement. But there was even more to this type—the scapegoat itself showed a type of the resurrection. It showed the living Christ—while one goat died, the scapegoat lived! It took the sins of the people upon it, and went off into the wilderness (Leviticus 16:21). Thus, the prophecy of the high priest each year was connected to the death and resurrection of the Lord Jesus! All of this comes together to beautifully show the prophecy which John brought out of Caiaphas' words.

So it was that the council of the Jews—unconsciously fulfilling types and uttering a prophecy—made the decision to put the Lord Jesus to death.

> "Then from that day forth they took council together for to put him to death." John 11:53

Somehow, this news found its way to the Lord. Perhaps it was from one of those in the council who believed in him—perhaps Nicodemus. One cannot be sure. In some way, the Lord found out about their decision. Knowing that it was not yet his time to depart from this world, he instead departed from the area of Jerusalem.

Christ's Reaction

> "Jesus therefore walked no more openly among the Jews; but went thence unto a country near to the wilderness, into a city called Ephraim, and there continued with his disciples." John 11:54

The Lord departed from the Jews. He left Bethany and went out into the wilderness, into a city called Ephraim—meaning "fruitful." It was there that the Lord Jesus stayed until his final journey to Jerusalem. He had performed a miracle which was astonishing enough to cause all of the Jews to come together to determine what to do about him. Their determination was not favorable and the hour of his departing was near. Truly though there were twelve hours in the day, the night was nigh at hand.

The Parable

The story of Lazarus' resurrection shows the wrestling of a family through their faith. Things had fallen upon them that they could not understand, yet throughout their situation, they continued to cling to their faith and trust in the Lord Jesus. Eventually, that faith was vindicated and Lazarus lived once again. It is a story which warms the heart, which gives hope to dark times, and yet shows the stubbornness of the mind of man—though many had witnessed this miracle, there were still some who refused to believe. Beneath all of these powerful lessons and dramatic turns in the story, just as with the other signs, there is a parable. This parable will have a similar focus to the story—hope. It will clearly show forth that while times may be difficult and we may seem confused, the Lord Jesus will eventually come and end the sadness. He will appear to his disciples and turn their mourning into joy.

The parable begins with the stoning of the Lord Jesus Christ. Just like the parable of the man born blind, this narrow escape from death fits well with the death and resurrection of the Lord.

The Resurrection of Lazarus

> "Therefore they sought again to take him: but he escaped out of their hand, and went away again beyond Jordan into the place where John at first baptized; and there he abode." John 10:39-40

The Jews sought to take the Lord Jesus, yet they could not! He was supposed to die, but amazingly he was still alive. This is representative of his death and resurrection, just like with the parable of the man born blind—then, the Lord departed from Jerusalem, matching up to his ascension to heaven. It was during this time when he was apart from Jerusalem and separated from the faithful in Bethany that many came to believe on him.

> "And many resorted unto him, and said, John did no miracle: but all things that John spake of this man were true. And many believed on him there." John 10:41-42

The preaching of the Lord Jesus Christ was wonderfully successful at this time. This matches up beautifully with the gospel going forth into all the world and being accepted by many peoples and nations. This is the context of the parable of Lazarus' resurrection. The Lord Jesus died and was resurrected, he ascended to heaven, and the gospel went out to the world. All of those incidents paint the scene for the story of this family in Bethany.

Mary and Martha

When trying to determine who is represented by Mary and Martha, an examination of the details of the story is quite helpful. Keeping in mind the setting of the parable, notice these specifics:

- Mary and Martha were separated from the Lord
- He was far away from them and they were in such circumstances that they could not come to him
- They pleaded with him to come to them soon
- The Lord loved them
- They were full of faith
- They anxiously waited for him to arrive
- He waited two days (representing two thousand years?) to come to them

When putting together all of these ideas, it would seem as though Mary and Martha represent the faithful at the time that the Lord Jesus returns. They were looking for his arrival and they were faithful until he came. Yet not only so, but they also struggled with waiting for him—they went through the same type of trial that the faithful of every age go through! So often we find ourselves wondering why the Lord hasn't yet returned! The prophecies seem to indicate that he is at the door, the world continues to get worse and more openly evil, and the ecclesia needs his leadership. Yet still we have not seen him. At times, we too, just like the faithful sisters, can become discouraged—we wonder why he has not yet come. It is for times like this that we can remember the reason that the Lord delayed his coming in this story—it wasn't because he didn't want to be with the faithful sisters, and it wasn't because he didn't long to help. It was because he loved them. So it is with our situation. We anxiously wait for the Master to return and he doesn't delay because he enjoys watching our struggles, instead the delay is so that we might be made more ready for his Kingdom and that more people might have time to repent and turn to the Truth.

The Resurrection of Lazarus

> "The Lord is not slack concerning his promise, as some men count slackness; but is longsuffering to us-ward, not willing that any should perish, but that all should come to repentance." 2 Peter 3:9

Today, the Lord Jesus delays his coming so that man may continue to have the opportunity to repent. It is because of his love that he has not yet come.

These two sisters represent the faithful who are alive at the time of Christ. They were waiting and looking for his arrival—and finally they saw it. They were told by a messenger that the Lord had arrived—much as it will be for us.

Lazarus' Death

While the two sisters represent the faithful who are alive when Christ comes, Lazarus seems to represent something that is a bit different. Truly, he was part of that same beloved family and truly he was a disciple of the Lord Jesus Christ. However, unlike the sisters, he was not consciously awaiting the coming of the Lord. He was not looking for the Master. Instead, he was asleep—just as the dead in Christ. While the sisters represent the faithful who are *alive* at the coming of the Lord, Lazarus represents the faithful who are *dead* at the coming of the Lord.

The Lord Jesus Christ will return and will bring life to the dead and will gather up the living believers. All of those who were dead will be raised once again—and just like Lazarus, they too will still be bound with grave clothes. Mortality will still cling to them. Yet by the grace of God, just as Lazarus, they will hear the command, "loose him and let him go"—and they will be given the gift of immortality.

Council against Christ

In this parable, we see the faithful who are alive and the faithful who are dead being brought together at the coming of the Lord Jesus. Interestingly enough, one of the events which immediately follows this miracle very much seems to confirm this interpretation of the parable. If the coming of the Lord to Bethany represents the coming of the Lord to the world, just think about what happened next. The powerful religious rulers then came together to determine their strategy to stop the Master. Scripture predicts a similar type of situation after the Lord Jesus returns again:

> "Why do the heathen rage, and the people imagine a vain thing? The kings of the earth set themselves, and the rulers take counsel together, against the LORD, and against his anointed, saying, Let us break their bands asunder, and cast away their cords from us." Psalm 2:1-3

When reading this psalm further, it becomes clear that its final fulfillment is when the Lord Jesus is enthroned in Jerusalem (Psalm 2:6). After the Lord comes, destroys the Gogian host and proclaims that all nations must submit to him, the rulers of this world will not accept his proclamation favorably. In fact, guided by the wisdom of the Catholic church and many of their Protestant daughters, the rulers of the earth will choose to stand against the Lord Jesus—looking at him as "the Antichrist" rather than the Son of God.

The Resurrection of Lazarus

Human nature has always been the same. In the original narrative, the Jews refused to believe in the power of Christ and instead resisted him. In the future, the kings of the world will hear of all of the mighty miracles which are performed by the Master, and instead of acknowledging those miracles as the power of God, they will blaspheme the power of the Holy Spirit and say that those miracles are the power of "the Antichrist."

This council fits in beautifully with the parable. The parable is all about the second coming of the Lord Jesus Christ. It looks at the anticipation of the faithful as they wait for his return, the resurrection from the dead, and the resistance of the kings of the earth against him. May it remind us that while Mary and Martha wondered if the Lord truly would ever come, he did one day arrive. So it will be with us. One day, by the grace of God, we will see his coming. One day, we will be with him.

May we hold to that hope and keep it strong in our mind so that when dark times come, there will always be light.

Chapter 8
The Miracle of the Fish

Much had happened since the resurrection of Lazarus—the world had been changed. The shameful plans of the Jewish council had been put into action and the Lord had been crucified. Yet the grave could not hold him. After three days in the grave, the Lord Jesus was given life again. Two angels proclaimed the good news to Mary Magdalene and she, in fact, saw him that day (along with Mary his mother). Later on that evening, the risen Master then appeared to the disciples:

> "Then the same day at evening, being the first day of the week, when the doors were shut where the disciples were assembled for fear of the Jews, came Jesus and stood in the midst, and saith unto them, Peace be unto you." John 20:19

The disciples saw their Lord again! What a joyous occasion this was for them—when he was crucified, they had lost all hope, not knowing what had just taken place. They believed that he was the one who was going to redeem Israel—yet he had been slain. Now, he was alive again. He had conquered death. After this, he appeared to them again just eight days later. At his first appearance, Thomas had not been with them—now Thomas could put his fingers in the holes on the Lord's hands. Now he could put his hand in his side. Now Thomas could believe.

> "And after eight days again his disciples were within, and Thomas with them: then came Jesus, the doors

The Miracle of the Fish

being shut, and stood in the midst, and said, Peace be unto you. Then saith he to Thomas, Reach hither thy finger, and behold my hands; and reach hither thy hand, and thrust it into my side: and be not faithless but believing." John 20:26-27

This was the second time that he appeared to his disciples. They had seen the immortal Lord twice. Soon, he would appear to them again—this time in Galilee. This was what he had told Mary Magdalene and his mother Mary when he saw them for the first time—they needed to tell his disciples that he would meet them in Galilee.

"Then said Jesus unto them, Be not afraid: go tell my brethren that they go into Galilee, and there shall they see me." Matthew 28:10

One week after his resurrection and after the disciples had seen the Lord twice in Jerusalem, it appears as though they then went to Galilee. They now followed the words of the Lord in his message conveyed by Mary Magdalene. Thus, the next place where they are found is around the sea of Tiberias, or the sea of Galilee, waiting for the Lord to come to them.

"After these things Jesus shewed himself again to the disciples at the sea of Tiberias; and on this wise shewed he himself. There were together Simon Peter, and Thomas called Didymus, and Nathanael of Cana in Galilee, and the sons of Zebedee, and two other of his disciples." John 21:1-2

The disciples were together at the sea of Tiberias, waiting to see the Lord Jesus again. This would be the third time that they would see him in the resurrected

Glimpses of the Master

state. At this point, there were seven of them gathered together. One of them, Peter, made a sudden exclamation of his plans for the next few hours. He was going to go fishing. Yet this sudden exclamation seems a little bit odd—why did Peter spontaneously decide to go fishing? He hadn't seriously been out fishing since he had first been called by the Lord Jesus—what prompted him to go back to his old ways?

> "Simon Peter saith unto them, I go a fishing. They say unto him, We also go with thee. They went forth, and entered into a ship immediately; and that night they caught nothing." John 21:3

Peter had not seriously fished for the past three years. He had been with the Lord Jesus all of that time, and why did he now decide to go back? It just seems a bit strange—yet not only so, but even the last time when he fished, the Lord had given him a special commission:

> "For he was astonished, and all that were with him, at the draught of the fishes which they have taken: and so was also James, and John, the sons of Zebedee, which were partners with Simon. And Jesus said unto Simon, <u>Fear not; from henceforth thou shalt catch men</u>." Luke 5:9-10

The last time that Peter had seriously fished on the sea of Galilee, the Master had told them that they would no longer be fishers of fish—from that moment forward, they would catch men. They would become fishers of men—they were to be preachers. They had been given a new mission by the Lord Jesus Christ—what was it that caused Peter to then turn back to the sea? Why on that day, while he was waiting for the Master to come, did he

The Miracle of the Fish

suddenly choose to get into the boat and try to catch fish once again? Why go back to the old life?

Perhaps the last few weeks had been a bit more difficult for the weary disciple than is initially acknowledged. He had probably struggled through his faith after the Lord had been taken. No doubt memories of his denials were still fresh in his mind. No doubt guilt over these sins still plagued him. It could be that this was why Peter went back to fishing. He needed to get his mind on something else—as he waited, that's all that he could think of. How he wished he could be with Christ once again—here they were, waiting for him. When would he come? Peter longed to see the Master and longed to somehow get final closure for his grievous denials. Not only so, but when the women saw the angels on the resurrection morning, one of the angels had a special message for Peter. The angel specifically said that *Peter* needed to go into Galilee to see Christ:

> "But go your way, tell his disciples and <u>Peter</u> that he goeth before you into Galilee: there shall ye see him, as he said unto you." Mark 16:7

Peter was particularly singled out in the command to go to Galilee—this would have been quite significant for him. Clearly, the Lord Jesus had something which he specifically wanted to say to Peter. Peter needed to make sure that he went to Galilee. While standing there on the shore of the sea, Peter must have wondered what it was that the Lord wanted to say to him—more than likely knowing that it had to do with his denials. Waiting would have been agonizing—Peter was a doer, he didn't normally take time to wait, and on top of that, there was no place that he would rather be than with Christ. Yet now he was at the sea of Galilee, waiting for the Master.

As Peter anxiously looked for the Messiah to meet them, all around him were signs of his past life. Nearby was his boat, and this was the sea upon which he had always fished. He was with James and John, his partners in fishing (Luke 5:10). He was back in the same hills where he had lived with his family—all of these things were so familiar. Truly, he had come to these same places many times with the Lord and he had been with James and John and in his own boat with the Son of God as well (Luke 5:3), yet this time, the Master wasn't there. Probably for the first time in years, Peter was in his homeland without the Lord Jesus—without the one whom he loved most. He was apart from the Lord—just like he was on the night in which he denied that he ever knew him.

So many thoughts would have been spinning in this poor disciple's mind. He knew that the Lord Jesus was a man of forgiveness, he had been taught this lesson by him personally (Matthew 18:21-22). Yet how foolish he felt! He had said that he had been willing to die for the Master, and he demonstrated that willingness when he sought to save him that night in the garden (John 18:10-11), but afterwards he found his confidence and faith failing. Three times he had denied the Lord—not only denied him, but actually refused that he even *knew him*. Hadn't the Lord Jesus said that whoever denied him would be denied before the Father (Mark 8:38)? And the look of sadness that he had seen on the Master's face after that last denial…

> "And the Lord turned, and looked upon Peter. And Peter remembered the word of the Lord, how he had said unto him, Before the cock crow, thou shalt

The Miracle of the Fish

deny me thrice. And Peter went out, and wept bitterly." Luke 22:61-62

That look had not left his memory. He had denied the one that he loved. How could he stand again and speak personally with the Lord? Did Christ still even want him as a disciple? He was a traitor—how could anyone want a traitor in their midst? He had failed so miserably.

Now, with all of these thoughts swirling through his mind, there he waited. Sitting amongst things which were so familiar, yet he felt so alone. The situation was too much for him—it overwhelmed his senses and he couldn't handle it any longer. He had to stop thinking about his denials—he had to get his mind on something else. What better thing to occupy his thoughts than something which had once captured his love before? Thus, he went back to his occupation before he knew the Lord Jesus, back to when he was just a fisher, and not a fisher of men.

Perhaps this was why the other disciples went with him when he decided to go fishing. Could it be that they could hear the anguish in his voice? Maybe they went along with the miserable man in order to comfort him and make sure that he stayed safe—it was probably well known to all of them what Judas had done during his moments of despair.

Thus the disciples went out fishing. All night they toiled on the sea—using every trick they knew and going back to every "special spot" they remembered from when they were fishermen. Yet it was to no avail. They caught nothing. Peter's effort to distract his thoughts had instead been a small lapse of faith—going back to how he had been before he met the Lord Jesus. Not only was

Glimpses of the Master

this effort to distract his thoughts a small lapse in faith, but it may have also been quite unsuccessful. Toiling all night upon the sea may have been a vaguely familiar situation. It was the exact same thing that had happened *the very last time* that he had been fishing:

> "And Simon answering said unto him, Master, <u>we have toiled all the night, and have taken nothing</u>: nevertheless at thy word I will let down the net." Luke 5:5

Just as this fishing trip after Christ's resurrection, the last time that Peter had been seriously fishing, his net had come up empty all throughout the night. It would seem that Peter's mind would have been brought back to that last time—he would have been thinking about that instance on the sea of Galilee when the Lord Jesus had called him. The Master had told him to go out again and to try fishing once more. When he did, the net was filled with fishes, so much so that the net actually broke. Both James and John had to come over so that all of the fish might be brought to shore—one boat could not hold them all! Peter may have chuckled or smiled as he remembered the event. Yet then his thoughts would have stopped cold. Once again, his mind would have been brought back to his denials. What was it again that he had said to Christ in that same incident?

> "When Simon Peter saw it, he fell down at Jesus' knees, saying, Depart from me; for I am a sinful man, O Lord." Luke 5:8

"For I am a sinful man..." How true that must have felt to Peter at that moment! Yet his thoughts were far from what they had been on that day—never again would he say to his Lord, "depart from me." What he would give

The Miracle of the Fish

to have his Lord with him at that moment! He was a sinful man, truly, he knew it—and he couldn't seem to escape it. Whatever he did, his denials of the Master were before his face (cp. Psalm 51:3). Even though he sought a distraction in fishing, he could not get his mind off of what he had done.

Instead of dealing with his hurt and doubts in prayer, Peter turned to distraction—an easy choice to make, but not a wise one. May we remember the lesson in our times of hardship while we wait for the Lord to come. Though waiting may sometimes feel unbearable and though we may have so many gloomy thoughts, may we remember the forgiveness of the Lord and turn our hearts to him, knowing that his grace will cover those who confess their sin. Peter was about to learn this.

As the darkness began to wash away into the morning, a figure could be seen on the shore. It was unrecognizable, but eventually it spoke to the disciples:

> "But when the morning was now come, Jesus stood on the shore: but the disciples knew not that it was Jesus. Then Jesus saith unto them, Children, have ye any meat? They answered him, No." John 21:4-5

The unknown figure asked them if they had caught anything—their answer came back despondently, "No." Yet as they answered, they must have thought the question a bit odd—not specifically the question per say, but in fact, the greeting. The man had called them "children"—and the definition of the Greek word only seems to be connected to things that are young; it definitely means "children." In fact, in some places is it actually translated as "young child" (Matthew 2:8, Matthew 18:2, Luke 18:16). As the disciples heard

Christ's words, they must have wondered why the man had called them that—he couldn't actually think that they were children, could he?

We know that the figure on the beach was the Lord, yet the disciples had no idea. Clearly, the Master knew that the disciples were not children, but he specifically chose this word—perhaps because it aptly described the way that the disciples, namely Peter, had just acted (contrast to what he had called them just previously; John 20:17). He had sought to bury his thoughts in his old life, he had allowed his fears to push him back to fishing. In a gentle rebuke, the Lord, knowing that they had caught nothing, called them "children" and asked what they had caught. With a slight bit of shame, the disciples gave their response to Christ. As their answer arrived at the shore, surprisingly, the figure on the beach gave a reply.

Advice from Christ

> "And he said unto them, Cast the net on the right side of the ship, and ye shall find. They cast therefore, and now they were not able to draw it for the multitude of fishes." John 21:6

The reply came back to them in the form of advice. If they would just cast the net on the right side of the boat, they would catch something. Typically these words of advice would have sounded foolish in a seasoned fisherman's ears! The disciples knew how to fish and they knew what they were doing. They had fished all night and found nothing—it would seem clear that they were not going to find anything now. This had been the complaint when the Master had told them to do

The Miracle of the Fish

something similar to this on the last time that they went fishing. "Master, we have toiled all night and taken nothing..." Yet there was something different about this incident that made the advice of the man from the shore sound plausible—possibly it was the way that Christ had said the words or possibly it was because the disciples remembered what had happened on their last fishing trip. This time, these words did not sound foolish to them, and thus they cast the net on the right side.

The result was the same as it had been at the beginning of Christ's ministry. The net was suddenly full of fish—it was so full that they could not bring it into the boat! The advice from the man on the shore had proved correct! How could that be? How had he known? As the disciples sought to pull in the net—baffled by what had just taken place before them—one of the disciples, John, realized what they had witnessed. They had seen a miracle. That figure on the shore wasn't *just* any man—it was the Lord Jesus Christ. The Master had come, their waiting was over.

> "Therefore that disciple whom Jesus loved saith unto Peter, It is the Lord. Now when Simon Peter hear that it was the Lord, he girt his fisher's coat unto him, (for he was naked,) and did cast himself into the sea." John 21:7

Suddenly it came together for John. This could only have taken place if Divine power was involved. The man on the shore must be the Lord Jesus—the circumstance was too similar to what had happened in Luke 5 for this to have been an accident. The Master was on the beach.

The disciples had toiled on the sea all throughout the night—Peter, turning to a worldly distraction to calm his mind—and they had caught nothing. The distraction had failed miserably. Not only might he have been reminded that he was a sinner, but he had also gone back to his old life. Now, as the sun was rising upon the sea, Peter, along with the rest of the disciples, was taught a powerful lesson. Turn to the Lord Jesus. Without him, all of our efforts are in vain. He knew where to find the fish—when the professional fishermen were at a loss, the Master knew! Not only so, but even greater than knowing where the fish were, he knew how to set Peter's mind at ease! In any circumstance, turn to the Lord. Other things in this world—the TV, the internet, the radio, video games—may vie for our attention and may seem to be a good distraction for the hurt or disappointment that we feel. But they aren't. May we instead fall on our knees before God in prayer. May we acknowledge that all of our efforts depend on Him.

As soon as John realized who it was that was on the shore, he turned to Peter and gave him the news. He knew that Christ had wanted to speak to Peter, and he probably knew the turmoil that was going on inside of Peter's mind. Lovingly, John turned to Peter and said "It is the Lord."

This was exactly what Peter wanted. He had been waiting for Christ, he had been wondering if the Lord still wanted him, and now the Master had come. His Messiah was there! There was no other place that he would rather be than with the Lord. He couldn't wait for the boat to get to shore. The other disciples were already struggling with trying to pull all of the fish into the boat—and it was taking too long! Peter's Messiah

The Miracle of the Fish

was on the shore! As long as Christ had been away, Peter had been in agony! He couldn't wait any longer. As quickly as he could, he put on his coat—not wanting to appear inappropriately before Christ. Suddenly, and probably to the surprise of all of the other disciples, Peter jumped into the water, swimming *with his coat on,* toward the Lord Jesus.

What a beautiful picture of discipleship this is. Leaving all of things of the past behind, Peter launched into the water. The monetary value of the fish and any of the emotional ties that he had once had for fishing were replaced by a passionate love for the Lord—yet in all of his passion, he was not disrespectful. He would not appear before the Lord naked. After the fall in the garden, nakedness became connected to shame:

> "And the eyes of them both were opened, and they knew that they were naked; and they sewed fig leaves together, and made themselves aprons." Genesis 3:7

As soon as Adam and Eve realized that they were uncovered—that they were naked—they made a covering for themselves. They were ashamed of their nakedness! Contrast this to before they had eaten of the fruit.

> "And they were both naked, the man and his wife, and were not ashamed." Genesis 2:25

Before they had eaten the fruit, both of them were naked and they were not ashamed. Yet after they had eaten it, suddenly they made a covering for themselves! The contrast presented here seems to indicate that as soon as they realized they were naked, they were ashamed of it! Again, another connection with nakedness and shame is given in the account of the golden calf.

> "And when Moses saw that the people were naked; (for Aaron had made them naked unto their shame among their enemies:)." Exodus 32:25

When worshipping the golden calf, the people were naked—and Scripture specifically denotes that being naked in this way was shameful! Thus, nakedness is associated with shame (see also 2 Chronicles 28:19, Isaiah 20:4). While Peter was not necessarily shamed about his own nakedness in front of the other fishers, this was not the way in which he wanted to appear before his Lord.

Before he went towards Christ, he put on his coat. Even though this meant that he would have to swim with his coat clinging to him, to be clothed before Christ was more important. He longed to be with him, but he would not appear before the Lord inappropriately. Though he had a familiarity with the Son of God, he did not forget the status of the man to whom he was swimming.

Leaving everything behind, Peter came closer and closer to the Lord. Even though he had fallen—in his denials and with the fishing that night—he put those things behind and pressed toward the mark. He set his eyes on the Lord Jesus and went towards him with all of his might. May this be an example for us. Even when our sins drag us down, may we get back up and continue to strive towards the Lord—and may we strive with reverence and respect.

The Miracle of the Fish

What would Peter have been thinking as he swam towards the Master? Would he still be musing of his denials? Would he be wondering what the specific message was that the Lord Jesus had for him? He would not have much longer to wait before his questions would be answered.

Meanwhile, the other disciples were still working with the fish. Upon realizing that they could not get them all into the boat, the disciples chose to drag the net to shore.

Coming to Shore

> "And the other disciples came into a little ship; (for they were not far from land, but as it were two hundred cubits,) dragging the net with fishes." John 21:8

The disciples made their way toward the shore, dragging their net behind them. The weight of the fish was too much, it couldn't be put in the boat. Once they finally reached the land, they found the Lord Jesus there with a fire prepared, a fish being cooked, and bread.

> "As soon then as they were come to land, they saw a fire of coals there, and fish laid thereon, and bread." John 21:9

The Master had prepared a meal—this was the mighty power of the one before them. He hadn't needed to toil all night on the sea, his net had not come up empty. The Master has all power in heaven and earth at his disposal—and while our efforts may sometimes prove futile, let us not forget the mighty power of the Father and the son. The Lord had prepared this meal and was there waiting for the disciples—at this point, John added another purposeful and important detail. He specifically mentioned that the fire was *"a fire of coals."* This Greek word, Strong's G439, only occurs in one other place in all of the New Testament—during the denials of Peter.

> "Then saith the damsel that kept the door unto Peter, Art not thou also one of this man's disciples? He saith, I am not. And the servants and officers stood there, who had made a <u>fire of coals</u>; for it was cold: and they warmed themselves: and Peter stood with them, and warmed himself...And Simon Peter stood and warmed himself. They said therefore unto him, Art not thou also one of his disciples? He denied it, and said, I am not. One of the servants of the high priest, being his kinsman whose ear Peter cut off, saith, Did not I see thee in the garden with him? Peter then denied again: and immediately the cock crew." John 18:17-18, 25-27

It's almost as though the fire of coals was an integral witness to Peter's denials. The first denial took place, and then Peter went over to the fire. At the fire, he gave his second denial. The third denial happened at the same place—where Peter "warmed himself." Now, Peter arrived at the shore after swimming two hundred cubits through the sea with his coat. As he rushed up the shore to see his Lord, he would have been struck by what he saw—a fire of coals. Since the word is only used in these two chapters of John, it seems clear that the apostle wanted his readers to make this connection. Peter saw the fire of coals and his mind probably jumped back to the last time that he had stood around a similar fire—that terrible night would not leave him in peace. Everywhere he went, it seemed as though it was

The Miracle of the Fish

being brought back to his attention. But now, things were different—he had come to the Messiah.

Even though Peter still had the memory of his denials looming before him, he was now with Christ. This was where he wanted to be. No longer would he turn back to fishing, no longer would he go back to his old life. He loved his Savior and desired to be with him. Just being in his presence filled him with strength.

> "Jesus saith unto them, Bring of the fish which ye have now caught. Simon Peter went up, and drew the net to land full of great fishes, an hundred and fifty and three: and for all there were so many, yet was not the net broken." John 21:10-11

The Lord Jesus gave a command—"bring of the fish which ye have now caught." Without needing further clarification, Peter was off. He went down to the shore, passed the boat, and took hold of the net. He then singlehandedly drew the net onto the land. These were the actions of a man who had been energized and changed by the presence of the Master. Earlier, the net was too full for it to fit onto the boat (John 21:8)—thus, the whole crew of disciples did what they could by dragging the net behind the boat. Now, Peter came to the net and pulled it up onto the land—by himself! This was an amazing feat of strength—and one which was accomplished by a man who had been given a command by Christ and who was going to do whatever it took to fulfill his mission. He had been reinvigorated by seeing the Lord.

All together, there were one hundred and fifty-three fish. They were all great fish, and despite their size, the net was not broken.

> "Jesus saith unto them, Come and dine. And none of the disciples durst ask him, Who art thou? knowing that it was the Lord. Jesus then cometh, and taketh the bread, and giveth them, and fish likewise. This is now the third time that Jesus shewed himself to his disciples, after that he was risen from the dead." John 21:12-14

The invitation now came forth to all of the disciples—"come and dine." They all readily agreed. They knew that the invitation had come from the Lord.

Peter's Test

After the meal was over, Peter's time had come. He had longed to have the Lord give him closure in this way for a while. Now the Master was about to speak to him about the denials.

> "So when they had dined, Jesus saith to Simon Peter, Simon, son of Jonas, lovest thou me more than these? He saith unto him, Yea, Lord; thou knowest that I love thee." John 21:15a

When they had all finished eating, Christ turned to Peter and asked him of his love—bringing the disciple's mind right back to the boast that he had made before Christ had told him of the denials. "Lovest thou me more than these?" The Lord asked him the question, probably signaling at the other disciples—that had been Peter's boast, that he loved the Lord more than all the others did.

The Miracle of the Fish

"Peter answered and said unto him, <u>Though all men shall be offended because of thee, yet will I never be offended</u>. Jesus said unto him, Verily I say unto thee, That this night, before the cock crow, thou shalt deny me thrice." Matthew 26:33-34

Peter had boasted to Christ that even though all of the other disciples turned and forsook him, he never would. Thus, the Lord responded to him by telling him of his denials. Now, after the event, the Master was calling his mind back to that night. Could he still look on all of the other disciples and make that boast? Could he honestly say that he had not acted in the same way that all of them had?

How it must have hurt Peter to have this asked to him. He knew that in his fear and confusion he had gone against what he said that night. Thus, he had to admit that his love was not as great as he had thought it was. When the Lord asked him the question, the Master used the word "agapao" for "lovest." As mentioned in an earlier chapter, this is the word that is connected to actions and *doing* loving things—ultimately, willing to die for someone else. This adds another dimension to the Lord's question. He was asking if Peter still believed that he was willing to die for his Messiah—and if he was willing to do so more than all of the other disciples were willing.

To this question, Peter had to answer "no." Yet this was not the kind of answer that Peter could bear to give to his Lord—truly, he *loved* him and he had been willing to die for him. His willingness to singly rush into a troop of Roman soldiers and attack one of the servants in order to save the Lord seems to demonstrate this—but Peter was too ashamed of his later failings. There had been points at which he had not be willing—and so he probably didn't feel as confident about affirming his "agapao" for Christ. Yet not wanting to say "no," Peter instead responded with an affirmation of a different kind of love. "Yea, Lord; thou knowest that I love thee."

In this response, Peter did not use the word "agapao," but instead used the word "phileo." He had an affection for Christ. To this he could testify—had not he just jumped into the sea with his coat on in order to see the Master? Clearly, he could confirm his affection for the Lord. Thus, that was his answer—surely it was not the type of answer that he would have wanted to give, but with the memories of his denials swirling through his mind, he could do no better.

In a beautiful response, the Lord Jesus showed Peter the grace of our God.

> "...He saith unto him, Feed my lambs." John 21:15b

Even though Peter would have been at least slightly ashamed of his answer, the Lord Jesus responded with inspiring words. Peter was to feed his lambs. Though he had denied him, though he had felt as though he were a traitor, Peter was still wanted by the Master. What a feeling of relief would have washed over Peter as he heard these words. He could still be a disciple. He could still follow the one whom he loved. Yet not only was this an indication to Peter that Christ still wanted him as one of his disciples, it was actually a reaffirmation of the original mission which the Lord Jesus Christ had given to him. Earlier in his ministry, after Simon's beautiful confession of faith, the Lord Jesus had given Peter a promise:

The Miracle of the Fish

> "And I will give unto thee the keys of the kingdom of heaven: and whatsoever thou shalt bind on earth shall be bound in heaven: and whatsoever thou shalt loose on earth shall be loosed in heaven." Matthew 16:19

This idea of the "keys of the kingdom of heaven" was a reference to the leadership in preaching that Peter would have. He would be the one who would "unlock" the kingdom of heaven to the Jews—which he did when he preached the Truth to them on Pentecost. Later, he would then be the one who would "unlock" the kingdom of heaven to the Gentiles—which he did when he preached to Cornelius. These keys were intimately connected to Peter's role of preaching. It was this preaching work which the Lord Jesus confirmed when he said to Peter, "Feed my lambs."

After his denials, Peter may have thought that he lost all of these privileges that the Lord had given to him earlier. He may have thought that the keys were taken from him. Now, the Master reaffirmed that he wanted Peter to be the one to do the feeding. He wanted Peter to be the preacher of righteousness—and he specifically connected this commandment back to the promise of the keys through the name that he called Simon—"Simon, son of Jonas." Rarely was Simon ever called by his father's name, but he was that day on the sea of Galilee (John 21:15, 16, 17) and also when he was given the keys (Matthew 16:17).

This first question by the Master would have been difficult for Peter, but the answer from Christ would have calmed his spirit. Then, the Lord asked him the same question a second time.

> "He saith to him again the second time, Simon, son of Jonas, lovest thou me? He saith unto him, Yea, Lord; thou knowest that I love thee. He saith unto him, Feed my sheep." John 21:16

It was almost the exact same question—but this time the Master dropped the "more than these." Again, Peter had the same answer. He knew that he could not answer affirmatively. Thus, he replied by saying that he "loved him," again with the word "phileo." He had an affection for Christ. Perhaps then he expected a similar answer from the Master—and he received one. Yet the answer which was given at this second question had a slight difference to the first answer, and this difference changed the meaning. In the first question, Peter had been told to "feed Christ's lambs," and the word for "feed" seems to be more connected to the physical act of feeding. Peter had been commanded to give food to Christ's lambs—to spread the spiritual food to those who were just learning the Truth. This was something that Peter would have been glad to do and something which he could aptly do once the power of the Holy Spirit came upon him. However, this second command was a bit different. There, the Lord Jesus used a word which was more connected with shepherding—it was a word which described the role of an elder in the ecclesia. This was a word which denoted pastoring, leading, guiding, supporting, and encouraging—not just teaching. Whereas the first word is never used in relation to the role of an elder in the ecclesia, this word is (see Acts 20:28, 1 Peter 5:2). This word describes the way that the Lord Jesus will work with the saints and with Israel when he comes again (see Matthew 2:6, Revelation 7:17). It's connected to shepherding—tending to the flock and caring for them.

The Miracle of the Fish

Peter's first commission from Christ was to go and feed the lambs. He was to give them spiritual food. Now, this second commission was even greater. He needed to be the shepherd. He was to be a leader in the Master's ecclesia. While the first command may have excited Peter and helped him to realize that Christ still wanted to work with him, the second may have been more intimidating—Peter had just served as the shepherd for the rest of the disciples, and his shepherding didn't end in the best way. He had led them back to the sea and back to their old lives. This was not the role of a good shepherd. Nevertheless, this was the job to which the Master called him—and he would need to learn to be a strong and faithful shepherd.

Perhaps after this second question, Peter thought that the questioning was finished—but the most heart-wrenching of all of the questions was yet to be asked.

> "He saith unto him the third time, Simon, son of Jonas, lovest thou me? Peter was grieved because he said unto him the third time, Lovest thou me? And he said unto him, Lord, thou knowest all things; thou knowest that I love thee. Jesus saith unto him, Feed my sheep." John 21:17a

Three questions and three affirmations to cover three denials. Yet this final question was the one which drove Peter to grief. In the previous two cases, the Lord had asked him if he had "agapeo" love toward him—love which was willing to die for the other. Peter honestly answered and said that he did not, rather, he had "phileo" or a loving affection for the Master. Now, with this final question, the Lord even questioned his "phileo" love. When Christ said "lovest thou me?" the third time, the word for love was "phileo." It was almost as though the Master was even questioning Peter's affection for him—asking Peter to look deep inside and see if he really even had that.

This final question made Peter grieve. He became sad at Christ's words—he had thought that even though he could not admit to having a love which would die for the Lord, at least he could say that he loved to be around him, he loved to hear his words. Now Christ had asked him if he truly felt that way—and what would he say? It was true that he had demonstrated his affection as he swam to shore, but hadn't his denials taken him to the point of denying that he *even knew* who Christ was? What could he answer? On that fateful night, not only had he not showed "agape" love, but he had also not shown "phileo" either. Full of shame and sadness, Peter replied to Christ:

> "And he said unto him, Lord, thou knowest all things; thou knowest that I love thee. Jesus saith unto him, Feed my sheep." John 21:17b

He could not hide anything from the Master. "Thou knowest all things." Even though Peter had not demonstrated his affection and care for Christ on that passover night, he *knew* that he loved his Messiah. Despite his denials, he could not deny his affection for his Master. He never wanted to leave him. Thus, he invited the Lord Jesus Christ to look inside of his heart—to look inside and see that he truly did have that "phileo" love.

The Master gave an answer of love and mercy. Once again, now for the third time, Peter was given the commission to feed Christ's sheep. Though he had faltered and though his faith had failed, the Lord Jesus still wanted him as a disciple—and still wanted him to be a shepherd over his flock. He had been forgiven. The love of God and the Lord Jesus Christ washed over the repentant Peter and called him to a high calling. He had been forgiven and was now to move on. Yet the mercy of God did not end there. The Lord's words were not yet finished:

> "Verily, verily, I say unto thee, When thou wast young, thou girdedst thyself, and walkedst whither thou wouldest: but when thou shalt be old, thou shalt stretch forth thy hands, and another shall gird thee, and carry thee whither thou wouldest not. This spake he, signifying by what death he should glorify God. And when he had spoken this, he saith unto him, Follow me." John 21:18-19

Oh the depths of the mercy of Christ! All throughout the denials, Peter had been reluctant to say that he had "agape" love for Christ—he couldn't say that he would truly die for him. No doubt Peter longed to say it—he had a passion for his Messiah. He would have burned to say that he would die for him—but after the denials, he didn't feel worthy to say it. Thus, the Master said it for him. After Peter's third affirmation of his affection, he had reached closure for his sin, and had shown that he had the humility to learn from his mistakes. No longer would he claim to have greater love than the other disciples. He had been humbled. Yet the Lord was about to do something for him that Peter never would have expected. Though Peter didn't feel himself worthy to claim that he would go to death for Christ, though he didn't think that he could claim to have "agape" love, Christ confirmed that Peter did. When he was old, another would gird him and would carry him where he would not. In this death, he would glorify God. He would die for Christ—he would have "agape" love.

What joy these words would have brought to a heart which had been so troubled. Throughout all of life's trials, he would remain faithful to the end and he would demonstrate his true self-sacrificing love. This was all that Peter wanted. Thus it was that his debt was cleared and he went on to truly shepherd the people of God. Later on in life he seemed to make reference to this charge of the Lord Jesus as he passed it on to the other ecclesial elders:

> "<u>Feed the flock of God</u> which is among you, taking the oversight thereof, not by constraint, but willingly; not for filthy lucre, but of a ready mind." 1 Peter 5:2

As he grew older, he passed on his charge to those who would lead the other ecclesias. Just as Christ had commanded him to feed his sheep, so must the elders of the ecclesias. But this isn't the only reference which Peter later made to that conversation with Christ. In his final epistle, Peter wrote a small comment which seems to indicate that he never forgot that the Master told him he would be faithful until the end:

> "Yea, I think it meet, as long as I am in this tabernacle, to stir you up by putting you in remembrance; knowing that shortly I must put off this my tabernacle, <u>even as our Lord Jesus Christ hath shewed me</u>." 2 Peter 1:13-14

Perhaps when writing this last letter, the aged apostle was thinking of what the Lord had told him at that meeting on the shore of Galilee.

The Miracle of the Fish

After all of the events of the previous night and now the new day, Peter had been forgiven. He had been commissioned by the Master to go forth and preach—to use the keys which he had been given to bring the gospel to the Jews and the Gentiles. Peter would do this with gladness, working in service for the one whom he loved most—and throughout all of this work, he would not forget the events of that third meeting with the Lord Jesus Christ.

The Parable

All of the events of the final sign come together to show a parable that brings a beautiful ending to the gospel of John. In the sign, the story of the judgment can be seen—yet not the judgment as we typically think of it. This final parable creates a picture of the judgment, but only the positive side of it. The picture presented here ignores those who are rejected at the judgment seat—instead, it focuses on those who have been made righteous and given immortality.

The context is that the disciples are out upon the sea while they are waiting for the Lord. They are together in the boat and it is night time. They have not caught anything. Many of these symbols have been seen before. Just like the parable in the walking on the water, these disciples in the boat represent the ecclesia. They are upon the sea of nations and they are seeking to be fishers—yet they are seeking in vain. They are seeking to catch fish without first consulting with Christ—they have not turned their fishing over to God. Thus, their nets come up empty. Only when they are given the help of the Lord do they catch any fish. This is not to say that no good "fish" will be caught by the ecclesia until

Christ returns—rather, it is again affirming the lesson that it must be recognized that our preaching is a work of God and that it is Him who gives the increase. Only through Him will our efforts succeed. Only through Him will any fish be caught.

A Draught of Fish

Early in his ministry, the Lord Jesus told a parable about a net—and this parable helps to quickly connect this story to the final judgment:

> "Again, the kingdom of heaven is like unto a net, that was cast into the sea, and gathered of every kind: which when it was full, they drew to shore, and sat down, and gathered the good into vessels, but cast the bad away. So shall it be at the end of the world: the angels shall come forth, and sever the wicked from among the just, and shall cast them into the furnace of fire: there shall be wailing and gnashing of teeth." Matthew 13:47-50

The Lord's parable was about a net which was cast into the sea and gathered fish. Once it was full, it was taken to shore and the fish were sorted—the good fish were kept and the bad fish were removed. This he likened to the judgment at the end of the world. It's a similar story to that which appears in John 21—except there was one major difference. In John's final sign, there is no sorting of the fish—all of them were "great fishes" (John 21:11). They were the kind of fish that people would want to keep. Though the picture given by John symbolized the judgment, it only symbolized the judgment of the righteous. There is no sorting or casting away of any of the fish. All of them are great,

The Miracle of the Fish

and none of them are lost. This conclusion is reinforced by the fact that John specifically mentioned that the *net did not break* when the fish were hauled to the shore (John 21:11). None of the fish went back into the sea—all of them stayed in the net.

This also lends an explanation to why John specifically gave a number to the amount of fish which were caught. When Peter brought up the net, there were one hundred and fifty-three fish. This number does not seem to appear anywhere else in Scripture—making it extremely hard to place any kind of meaning upon it. Many good Bible students have sought to come up with some kind of symbolic significance for the one hundred and fifty-three, and have found much difficulty in the task. However, perhaps the fact that it doesn't specifically have a symbolic explanation is the exact point—it is a number to which we do not have a meaning, our understanding cannot place it. The one hundred and fifty-three fish represent those who are given eternal life at the judgment—a number which no man knows. However, the number is known to the Father.

> "Blessed be the God and Father of our Lord Jesus Christ, who hath blessed us with all spiritual blessings in heavenly places in Christ: <u>according as he hath chosen us in him before the foundation of the world</u>, that we should be holy and without blame before him in love." Ephesians 1:3-4

God knows all those whom He has chosen. He knows those who will be in His Kingdom—He declares the end from the beginning (Isaiah 46:10)! While we do not know the exact number of the righteous, our Father does. He knows exactly how many will be in His kingdom, and that is why the parable is given a specific number—yet the number is purposefully one which we cannot understand. This way, it can be remembered that God is the one who knows the number of the righteous—not us.

The picture of the net is a picture of the judgment, but only one side of the judgment. It shows a picture of those who are deemed righteous and given eternal life. After this picture and after the fish have been caught, the disciples came together with the Master to share a meal, much as the righteous will in the Kingdom of God.

Peter's Affirmations

With the picture of the judgment being finished, it is almost as though Peter's threefold affirmations to Christ are an extra appendix to the parable. They tend to show an extra element, as though to give a bit of a picture themselves as to how the judgment of the righteous will be. Though they struggled and though they failed many times, the true question is—did they love the Lord Jesus Christ? Such was the test for Peter. Yet at times, believers may even find it hard to answer that question, just as the apostle Peter did. Ultimately, at that judgment, it must be said, "Lord, thou knowest all things..." And the Lord Jesus will look into our hearts to see if that love for him is there. May we all pray that at that day, he might find what he is looking for. By the grace of God, he will. May we seek to foster that love in all that we do—reading through the Word of God, staying constant in prayer, and spreading the good news.

Epilogue

As the apostle John wrote, all of these signs were written for a particular purpose.

> "And many other signs truly did Jesus in the presence of his disciples, which are not written in this book: but these are written, <u>that ye might believe that Jesus is the Christ, the Son of God; and that believing ye might have life through his name</u>." John 20:30-31

The purpose of all of the signs was to show that Jesus is the Christ. John's gospel could have been filled with all of the different miracles that were recorded by Matthew, Mark, and Luke. However, John had a particular purpose in the things that he recorded. In all of these signs, he wanted his readers to see the power and majesty of the Lord Jesus Christ, and to recognize his glory. Thus, each of these recorded miracles is something special, something which which was so rare, that its occurrence would prove that Jesus was the son of God—never before had someone turned water into wine, never before had someone walked on the water. Each of these signs comes together in a beautiful picture to show that the Lord Jesus is truly the Messiah sent from God—a man who was and is unparalleled in all of history.

Yet there was more.

In believing that Jesus is the Christ, John sought to make it possible for his readers to have life —"and that believing ye might have life though his name." His was a gospel focused on bringing life to the world, one which sought to show that Jesus, the son of God, is the one who came to the world to bring life to those who were living in death. Constantly throughout the gospel of John this comes up as a theme:

"That whosoever believeth in him should not perish, but have <u>eternal life</u>. For God so loved the world, that he gave his only begotten Son, that whosoever believeth in him should not perish, but have <u>everlasting life</u>." John 3:15-16

Those who believed in Christ would have everlasting life—this is twice emphasized by John in these two verses. This theme comes up over and over. Again, in the same chapter:

"He that believeth on the Son hath <u>everlasting life</u>: and he that believeth not the Son shall not see life; but the wrath of God abideth on him." John 3:36

It's the same message, written just a few verses later—the Lord Jesus Christ brings life. Once more, when speaking to the Jews, the Lord said the same thing:

"And ye will not come to me, that ye might have <u>life</u>." John 5:40

These were the words of the Lord to the Jews—many of them refused to come to him and as a result, they would not have life. Life comes through the Master.

"The thief cometh not, but for to steal, and to kill, and to destroy: I am come that they might have <u>life</u>, and that they might have it more abundantly." John 10:10

Epilogue

The Lord Jesus had come so that his sheep might have life—this is something which John sought to bring to his readers. Life could only come through Christ—thus, all throughout his gospel, he emphasized this. Therefore, though the purpose of the signs was to show his readers that Jesus is the Christ, the son of God—it was through this realization and through believing it that Christ's followers might *have life in his name*. The purpose of John's signs was to bring his readers to life! Thus, when bringing together all of the parables in his gospel, this theme of life can be seen throughout. The interpretation of all of the parables shows that the Lord Jesus is the life, that life must come through him, and that some would reject this life while others would accept it. Note this common theme throughout all of the parables:

1. The water into wine - Christ brought new teaching and this new teaching would bring *life* in God's kingdom.

2. The healing of the nobleman's son - When they turn to him, Christ will bring *life* to Israel (John 4:51)

3. The healing of the invalid - The Jews were offered *life* through Christ and rejected it (John 5:40)

4. Feeding of the five thousand - Christ gave of himself in order to bring *life* to a multitude (John 6:33)

5. Walking on the water - Christ will arrive in the midst of turmoil and brings *life* to the ecclesia

6. The healing of the man born blind - Christ offered *life* to the Gentiles and they graciously accepted it (cp. John 8:12)

7. Resurrection of Lazarus - Christ will give *life* to those who sleep (John 11:25)

8. The miracle of the fish - The Lord will give eternal *life* to all of the "great fish" in his net

Each of these signs tells the story of Christ being the one who brought life—life can only come through him. This seems to be the purpose which John sought to show with the parables beneath the signs—the Lord Jesus is the life. This is a particular and purposeful contrast to Moses—while Moses stood for the same principles and stood for the same God, his law was given for the purpose of bringing the Jews to Christ (John 5:46, Galatians 3:24). The law of Moses was not the final testimony or the final revelation of God—it was given for the purpose of teaching Christ's principles and bringing its followers to faith. Yet many of the Jews never recognized this. Instead, for them it became a system of laws to follow in order to earn life—but that was not possible. Life could not and cannot be earned. This was the crowning purpose of John's signs and parables—if one continued to walk in Moses and sought to earn life through his statutes, one would die. There was no life in the works of Moses. There was only life in Christ.

Thus, when writing all of these signs, John purposefully made a contrast between the Lord Jesus Christ and the prophet Moses. John recorded miracles of Christ which were all about life and all about life coming through the Lord. What a contrast this was to Moses, whose major miracles were all about destruction—Moses was known for the ten plagues, miracles which were completely and entirely focused upon the destruction of a nation. Yet

Epilogue

Christ's miracles were about life. It wasn't a coincidence that John recorded Christ's first miracle as water into wine and Moses' first major miracle was water into blood. It isn't a coincidence that Moses brought darkness upon all of Egypt, preventing the Egyptians from seeing, but Christ proclaimed that he was the light of the world while healing a blind man. While Moses brought divine destruction, Christ brought divine life.

Over and over through these signs, John sought to show his readers that the works of the law did not bring life—the old wine had failed. Life could only come through the Lord Jesus—thus all of the parables seek to show that same message.

May we remember this. While we do not have the temptation to follow the works of the law, may we remember the main thrust of the lesson—life cannot be found anywhere else, only in the Lord. While the rest of the world seeks for glory and honor through their careers, through their education, or through their status, may we remember that there is one who has brought true life —the Lord Jesus Christ. In recognizing this, may we be filled with a great thankfulness for this knowledge, a zeal to spread it to others, and a resolve to stand firm unto the end.

"For the law was given by Moses, but grace and truth came by Jesus Christ." John 1:17

Made in the USA
Middletown, DE
05 January 2023